Best to Kathy Glass — a hard-worker! Go inspire

KENTUCKY'S EVERYDAY HEROES even

more!

Steve Flairty

Hero Glass

Martha Elaine Sparks - p.109

To Kathy —
Best wishes
James B Stephenson

Kentucky's Everyday Heroes

Ordinary People
Doing Extraordinary Things

by Steve Flairty

Foreword by David Dick

Edited by Michael Embry

International Standard Book Number 978-1-893239-75-3
Library of Congress Control Number 2007942893

First Edition

Jacket design by Bryant Wells.

To my father, Eugene Flairty,

who showed me Kentucky at an early age;

to my mother, Alma Flairty,

who put up with my daydreaming—still, today.

Contents

Acknowledgments

When you write a book about a lot of people, you need a lot of helpful people in order for it to be successful. I had wonderful help, and I owe heaps of gratitude to the following:

Charlie Hughes, my publisher at *Wind Publications*, knows Kentucky's people as well as anyone, and he had been thinking about doing a book similar to this one. Almost accidentally, we joined forces and it has worked.

Mike Embry, formerly my editor at *Kentucky Monthly*, has made my writing look better than it deserves. It's good to find people whose experience vastly trumps mine—and who are willing to humbly offer some of it to a needful colleague.

I am appreciative, and inspired, by having such a distinguished chronicler of Kentucky life, David Dick, to write the foreword for *Kentucky's Everyday Heroes*. He'll never know the influence he's had on my literary endeavors.

Early on, KET's Bill Goodman was an encourager and introduced me to three "heroes" who are part of the book. David Hawpe, columnist for *The Courier-Journal*, was a huge catalyst in publicizing my need for hero nominations. Others who suggested plenty of names to consider for the book were Sara Turnbull, Guy Waldrop, George Wofford, Cathy Wachtel, Cleo Roberson, Steve Vest, Barbara Cissell, Jane Royster, Gloria Rie, and Bruce Singleton.

Along the way, people like my friend (and first-born hero) Tim Farmer, who was the subject of my first book, Roger Singleton, Suzanne Isaacs, Toni Taylor, Eric Fruge, Carl West, Theresa and Mike Flairty, and Terrence Cecil cheered me on.

Most importantly, I would like to thank my ordinary, everyday heroes scattered around Kentucky. You are the reason I wrote this book. You are extraordinary.

Foreword

When I returned, in 1955, from the Philippine Islands, following a four-year tour of duty with the U.S. Navy, I had a strong desire to become a California writer.

I would specialize in Kentucky stereotypes. They'd be my meat and potatoes. They'd be my passport to fame.

And why not? The hillbilly characters were there for the raucous laughing, the tasting of much better fruit—Hatfield and McCoys, and other feuds galore.

I would quickly tidy up my degree in English literature at UCLA, which I'd begun in 1948 at the University of Kentucky. I would sit at the table where the stereotypers feast.

I was one of those refugees from the L'il Abner, Daisy Mae, Moonbeam McSwine, Mammy and Pappy Yocum part of the nation. I would regale these stories and make lots of money watching sunsets spreading above Malibu.

I would tell the "truth" and who knows, I might have created "The Beverly Hillbillies." But, as luck would have it, UCLA would not accept me as a California resident, and I would have to pay out-of-state tuition, something I definitely could not afford.

So, I returned to the University of Kentucky and began to understand the real grassroots people of the Commonwealth, especially that brother and sisterhood of writers who see beyond the stereotypes.

Steve Flairty, author of *Kentucky's Everyday Heroes: Ordinary People Doing Extraordinary Things,* has done just that. He has captured the essence of what it means to be a Kentuckian with a heart and soul.

In this collection of portraits, reaching about six thousand miles traveled from Whitesburg to Paducah, Covington to Jamestown, Flairty has applied just the right touch to a canvas of selfless love, courage, and commitment to lasting values. The heroes are all there, and they're making a positive difference.

You'll meet Billy Edwards, a native of Henderson, who counters cerebral palsy with a religious column for *The Gleaner*. Flairty includes him in *Kentucky Heroes* because Billy "speaks eloquently and inspirationally with the printed word."

Jamie Vaught of Middlesboro: "After finding out that their infant son, Jamie, was nearly deaf, it quickly became a family project to provide all the support necessary for his optimal development. Jamie learned to lip read and studied hard in school. Today, Jamie Vaught is a college professor and a successful writer, authoring four popular books on Kentucky Wildcats' basketball and writing columns for several periodicals. He was also instrumental in KET's decision to use closed-captioned local newscasts for late rebroadcast."

Then there's Bennie Doggett of Covington: "This dynamic social worker, trained with 'life experiences' rather than formal college instruction, has no fear in fighting for better lives for her clients, who are often poor, often with addictions, and often uneducated. She recently came out of retirement to serve voluntarily at the Oasis Outreach Center in Covington, a creation of her home church. A Kentucky Post editor called her "…a sort of untrained social worker, lawyer and ombudsman/problem solver for poor people…a gem, a fighter and stubborn."

Steve Flairty's style is spare and clear as it is strong, making a solid reading experience for those who understand that there are countless Kentucky heroes living unselfish lives for the benefit of all.

The Al Capp notion of Kentuckians—barefoot and brainless—and Hollywood fiction invented by transplanted Californians, profit by the belief that violence and stereotypes make the cash registers ring.

But, in the words of Jim Lyon, Sr. of Greenup County: "My mother used to say 'My baby doesn't have any hands and doesn't have any leg, but he has a mind,' and that always sat well with me…I never dwell on the negatives."

Steve Flairty has dwelt on the positives. They ring true, and Kentuckians are all the richer for it—"celebrating the human spirit of compassion."

— David Dick, author of *Kentucky: A State of Mind,*
Rivers of Kentucky, and *The View from Plum Lick*

Introduction

I'll never forget when my younger brother, Mike, and I were small boys growing up in the tiny northern Kentucky communities of Grant's Lick, and later Claryville, my father insisted that our family's short vacation trips revolve around traveling our state. Mom would fix sandwiches and iced tea to take along, and we'd often sleep overnight in our Ford station wagon. It was fine with me; I didn't wish for places more exotic because the trips rescued me, for short periods, from time working in the family's tobacco crop—which I tried to avoid when possible.

It seems that Dad, before his two-year hitch in the Marine Corps started in 1951, had been employed by the Highland Construction Company to help pave roads throughout Kentucky. Those locations included isolated parts of eastern Kentucky and the wide open areas of the Pennyroyal in the western section, along with his native Bluegrass area and also southward towards the Tennessee border. Dad's job was hard work, he made us understand, but during his time with Highland, he developed a liking for the land he saw and the people he came to know. On our vacation trips, Dad often talked about those places and told of his friends he'd made. Sometimes, we even took the time to search for them off the main roads.

Later, Dad took a job driving a truck locally for a wholesale ice cream company, but he never lost his deep-seated sense of place, Kentucky-style. And in a real, abiding way, Dad's personal endearment for the state of Kentucky became mine also.

Today, after a career as a public school teacher and now a writer of Kentucky stories, my love for my homeland gets stronger as I age. It has become more than an interest and a hobby for me—it helps frame my worldview; it makes me look at things proudly from a Kentuckian's point of view. Certainly, our state has problems that we—together—need to tackle vigorously: health-related concerns, our economy, improved education and the environment are a few. But we also have a soul about us that other parts of the nation might do well to emulate.

So, with plenty of passion and a desire to shine the light on the Commonwealth's most precious resources—its people—I set out to find and write about some of our finest citizens. I call them Kentucky's everyday heroes. They're the extraordinary among the ordinary, often not well-known except in their local communities. They're people who inspire others by the way they live daily. They're like Kentuckians I had noticed all my life, or, at least, had a strong notion they were there. They go quietly about their daily living, making others' lives better, with little or no thoughts of personal benefit; they are people who deal courageously with private, almost overwhelming challenges, such as physical or mental disabilities, and do it with grace. There are many out there, and other Kentuckians need to know about them.

On this go-around, I've found forty people and have encapsulated them in thirty-seven stories. It's a good list, a good start, but certainly not an exhaustive one. It's not necessarily even a "top forty" list, but it's a great representation. I put 6000 miles on my 2001 Lexus, gathered about seventy-five hours of tape, and took over a year to do the project. Glad I did, 'cause I treated myself to forty of the most invigorating, uplifting encounters of my life.

Hope you will enjoy the same treat that I did.

— Steve Flairty

Kendall Harvey

Three-Wheel Offering

Several years ago Kendall Harvey retired from his vocation of building houses in Adair County, but he really didn't have a plan to keep him busy. He didn't fish or hunt, and he didn't particularly like watching TV. Though a Kentucky native, he wasn't even a big Wildcat fan. He wondered long and hard about how he would use his time, and even wondered if he did the right thing by retiring. So much that it began to get to him, like a bad itch or a nauseated stomach. One day, a chance meeting with a child with Down syndrome at a restaurant in Columbia turned Harvey in a different and remarkably rewarding direction.

"I looked at the little boy and asked him if he had a bike," Harvey said, "and he said, 'Yes, it was tore up and it was getting fixed.'"

The boy's mother looked at Harvey with knowing eyes. "He can't ride one," she said. "He just *told* you that."

"Well, he's getting ready to ride one," said Harvey, eyes twinkling. After retrieving a little more information about the child, Harvey went home and began to build a three-wheel bicycle. Within a week, the young boy was presented his new bike—sized up and adapted to his individual physical needs. For Harvey, the happy reaction from the child and mother was all he needed to start him on a gratifying retirement—one that has seen him build, with his own caring hands, more than 150 specially-adapted three wheelers for those with disabilities, mostly children.

"I don't charge a thing," Harvey said. "I just like to help little boys and girls like that."

He's been doing just that for the last seven years, toiling happily in his small, downstairs workshop in his Columbia home. By now, Harvey has a nice little system going. He receives donated bicycles from a local department store, which he takes apart and combines with other bike parts to make his own hybrid brand.

Kendall Harvey

"I used to buy most of the bikes from them, but I told them since I was giving bikes away, I wasn't going to pay for them anymore," he said. Other businesses give him scrap wood, metal and even pieces of carpet to do simple upholstering. With materials always available, Harvey is content to work his magic down in his small basement workshop.

"He sometimes stays down there a long time," his wife, Cecile, said with a grin. "He cares for everybody, and the Lord has given him the ability to do these things to help others."

Harvey has a photo album of the recipients with their bikes. He beams as he describes each one.

"I built this little girl one and put dolls on it. She outgrew them, then I put a radio on it," he said. Pointing to another picture, Harvey explained the boy's dreams: "This little fellow looks like he is about three, but he's really eleven. He wants to be a lawyer and he's sharp as a tack"

"See this one," Harvey said as he pointed to another photo. "She runs up and hugs me every time she sees me. One of the little boys, when he got his bike, said, 'Am I dreaming?' It made my day."

Rod and Carole Embry of Bowling Green saw their Down syndrome son, Alex, receive a red three-wheeler, his favorite color, from

Harvey. "Because of his selflessness, generosity, and genuine care for others, Mr. Harvey is a real hero in our eyes," Rod said.

Even more remarkable about Kendall Harvey is that he continues his loving and creative pursuit as he is burdened with the effects of brain surgery a few years ago. "I had been having lots of seizures, so they operated," he explained. "That kept me from having seizures, but I'm not thinking like I did before. The doctors said it will eventually get better."

The community around Columbia knows Harvey as one with a caring heart, but they also know of his adventurous spirit, particularly in his younger days. "I made my own paraplane," he said with a smile. The odd looking flying machine, which basically is a motorized three-wheeler with a parachute attached, was a progression of work Harvey did from his hang gliding days.

"One Fourth of July, I flew that thing right onto the front yard of the Columbia courthouse," Harvey said. "And on another Fourth, I flew it to the Jamestown courthouse." Asked if Cecile rode with him, she laughed and said, "No, somebody had to stay on the ground and pray." His three-wheeler flying days "are probably over now," he said.

Harvey and his wife are devoutly religious, and their youngest son ministers to a large church in the South. While Cecile teaches in their local Nazarene church that Kendall built forty years ago and he "hands out bulletins at services," it is clear Kendall Harvey demonstrates his faith most eloquently through his three-wheeler endeavor, which might rightly be called his "ministry." As long as he stays healthy, he sees "no change" in what he does. "I started and couldn't get stopped," he said, matter-of-factly.

And that's a good thing, because Harvey's fellow Kentuckians are truly blessed by his three-wheel offering.

Robbie Doughty

Soldier Shows Honor in Adversity

The Robbie Doughty story has "feel good" painted all over it, but it's full of hard substance, too. It acts as a model for lessons to be taught; it's about believing in others and believing in oneself. It's about optimism, bravery, and loyalty.

His story shows us that the best way to live is, in all things, honorably.

Staff Sgt. Doughty rode in the lead Humvee along the Samarra bypass, Iraq, on July 8, 2004. He sat on the passenger side, his wide eyes open for suspicious enemy activity as his unit performed intelligence work while heading out to visit one of the other teams. Two other vehicles in the convoy followed on this typically hot, summer day in a desert place far from the western Kentuckian's home.

The Paducah area native, a Lone Oak High School grad, had participated in Army Reserve basic training between his junior and senior years. He had been an Army recruiter stationed in Bowling Green. But now, in a different, dangerous environment, Doughty suddenly took the brunt of a roadside bomb explosion from Iraqi insurgents, detonated remotely, possibly by a cell phone. One of his boots was blown off, and the blow did obvious damage to his legs, but that was not his immediate concern.

"It felt like all of the air was suddenly sucked out of me and so I was just trying to breathe," Doughty recalled. Using correct military procedure, their convoy quickly sped ahead in order to escape the attacking insurgents zone. With the help of nearby U.S. attack helicopters, they soon were removed from more imminent danger, but for Doughty, more bad news was coming.

Photo: Fishman Public Relations

Two Special Forces medics raced to Doughty's side. Feverously, they worked to apply tourniquets, one medic doing one leg, one doing the other. The quick and heroic work saved the victim from bleeding to death, but in short time, at a combat surgical hospital in Balad, both legs were amputated. Doughty, who had dreamed of adventure and daring acts

Robbie Doughty

since his days in elementary school, was flown to Germany for four days of intense attention, then to Walter Reed Hospital in Washington, D.C. He had left a huge part of himself in Iraq.

"Sure, I knew there was always danger involved, but I never thought about losing my legs. I just wanted to do everything I could to prevent something like 9-11 from happening again," he said.

Another chapter, one of loving support began at Walter Reed. Doughty's mother and father came to stay with him as he began rehabilitating. Close by was Kristina, his fiancée. His younger brother, John, whom Doughty recruited for the Army and happened to be on leave from a tour in Afghanistan, was there. Close friend and fellow Special Forces intelligence officer Lloyd Allard kept in daily contact. Then, there was Tom Porter, a Korean War veteran who long ago lost his legs in battle and fell in love with his physical therapist—later to become his wife. Porter, by now in his seventies, showed up to support wounded Iraq veterans, something he had been doing for years, and took a particular liking to Robbie Doughty. The feeling was mutual.

"Tom really inspired me." Doughty said. "Here was a guy who lost his legs a long time ago and didn't let it keep him from a useful life."

The time at Walter Reed Hospital figured to be two years—a long and arduous two years of rehabilitation. He received two artificial legs and would be taught by therapists how to use his new limbs to walk again. Doughty remembered the challenges: "I had surgery eight times. Just when you got conscious and able to talk, it was back into surgery."

Almost miraculously, however, Doughty walked confidently out of the military facility on his two prosthetic legs in only five months and traveled home to Paducah to await a new direction in life.

Diane Doughty, his mother and constant encourager through the rehabilitation process, was not totally surprised by her son's remarkably quick and successful recovery. "Robbie was bound and determined to workout all the time, and he made me a little scared and nervous at times," she said. "He used to set goals back in the seventh grade, and he always did everything he said he'd do."

Lloyd Allard became good friends with Doughty some two months before Doughty was injured, and his admiration for him is profuse. "Robbie has such perseverance and willingness to stick to it," Allard said. "When he was being dispatched out on his assignment, he just got himself ready to go. He always does what he's supposed to do and doesn't complain about anything."

But there is more to tell about the stirring account of Doughty's challenges, and the way he faced them.

USA Today published a Thanksgiving 2004 inspirational feature on Doughty's experiences in the war and at Walter Reed. By chance, Michael Illitch read the article with great interest and admiration. Illitch is the owner and founder of the Little Caesar's Pizza chain, as well as owning the Detroit Red Wings hockey and Detroit Tigers baseball teams. He had served as a U.S. Marine and felt a strong appreciation of Doughty's upbeat attitude, courage, and love of country. After giving some consideration to the matter, Illitch contacted Doughty. His message to the Iraq War veteran was unusual, but generous and alluring to the young man who was recalibrating his life.

"Mr. Illitch offered to basically give me, free, a Little Caesar's franchise to run," Doughty said. "He said I might need to get a partner to help. I really liked the idea and it was a great thing for Mr. Illitch to do."

Doughty immediately brought to mind a person to join him in the venture—his close friend Lloyd Allard. Allard quickly agreed, and in January 2007, their Little Caesar's store opened in Paducah. The business has been very successful, and Allard and Doughty have plans to open another store in Clarksville, Tenn., Allard's home town. Doughty's brother, John, finished his active military recently and now works for Robbie at Little Caesar's. John plans to open a store in Murray.

And what is Robbie Doughty's business management style? "He is honest and intelligent," Allard said. "People know about Robbie and respect him for it. He's like he was in the Army, when he gives someone a task, he expects it to be done." A grinning Doughty answered the question by simply saying, "I try to keep all my employees happy."

After all, his employees know that any hardships they encounter likely pale in comparison to what Robbie Doughty has overcome.

To Kathy,
from Kathy

Kathy Parrott

Ms. Kathy's Real-life Class with Strings Attached

The observer walks into the classroom and immediately takes notice of a couple of medium-sized turtles swimming in aquariums, several cockatiels making happy sounds in their cages, a content looking chinchilla named Chester and an energetic family of goldfish. There are work tables, along with framed pictures of former and current students who have the look of confidence. There's a makeshift "store" that has both play and real money. Students, the teacher and teacher aides are scurrying around in an obviously purposeful frenzy, like something real important is about to happen any minute. Then, the observer sees a violin, made child-size and showing wear from heavy use.

His head spins with curiosity, even wonder.

Teacher Kathy Parrott, better known around the classroom as "Ms. Kathy," believes all, yes, *all* students can learn. Understand that she might need to use a healthy dose of unorthodox methods to prove her point, but it's easy to observe what good she's been doing in her classroom for grades one to five special needs students.

At Rosenwald Dunbar Elementary in Jessamine County, perhaps the most impressive result of her work is the forty or so students who, in the last several years, have learned how to play the violin, many of them good enough to be part of a school orchestra.

"We have a concert every spring, and the parents really come out for it," she said. "I even had a grandfather come out of the hospital for the concert. A nurse brought him in a wheelchair, and he was on oxygen. He wasn't going to be stopped from seeing his grandchild perform."

Creating excitement in her classroom is nothing new for the passionate educator. The violin project started when a student's parent came to Parrott and in-

Kathy Parrott

quired about her fourth grade daughter's desire to play a violin. "Is there anything that can be done? I hate to tell her no," said the parent. The energetic, always thinking, always for the underdog Parrott began to take action. She talked with the school's orchestra teacher, J. Matt LaBarbara, about the child's situation and the mother's frustration. Cut from the same cloth as Parrott in regard to believing all can learn and all have dignity, LaBarbara got busy, too.

Parrott's other students likewise showed interest in playing the strings instrument, so LaBarbara wrote an educational grant for a computer and software that would help him adapt the music book for ten special needs students. Consequently, he devised color codes, finger placements and note names that non-readers could understand.

Now with momentum on their side, the school's PTA purchased ten violins and Parrott's kids were on the way to achieving a goal many thought improbable for members of her class. Without a music background and recognizing a need for professional enrichment, Parrott proceeded to become a student herself. Alongside her students, she learned and practiced, garnering even more respect from them in the process. Confidence begat confidence, and a new and creative addition to Ms. Kathy's class grew. It was, and is today, both fun and disciplined work habits that both teacher and students demonstrate every-day.

The music program now established, Parrott points to the many benefits to her students. They've grown in personal responsibility by doing the chores of setting up chairs and music stands for practice and by maintaining their instruments in good order. Handwriting has im-proved as they gain in flexibility with their fingers. Reading music has translated to improved reading of words, and listening skills are better as attention spans have increased. The gains have added to overall self-esteem.

Additionally, the program has gotten more parents closely involved with their children's learning. For many of the parents, this is the first school based educational activity they have experienced. Every suc-cessful step in learning how to play the violin is celebrated. From learning to hold the violin properly to to performing a short song, each child is praised for their accomplishment.

Besides talking about her class's musicians, Parrott loves to tell the story of how the turtles came to live in her classroom. "My daddy found the eggs in a nest near a pond where a raccoon had been eating the newly hatched babies," she said. "He brought them to my class, we hatched sixteen of them and kept two. We released the rest into Hick-man Creek." The account of the four cockatiels and their health con-cerns demonstrates Parrott's intuitive sense of the "teachable moment"—of which she constantly seeks. "We found out from a vet that the birds needed shots, and that we could get a special deal for a total of fifty dollars. I told my kids that they could use the money we had to have a pizza party or take care of the birds. First, about half said let's have a pizza party." The teacher then put it another way. "I let them know that these birds were our 'kids'," and shouldn't we first take care of our kids?" The point was made, the birds got their shots—and real-life learning took place in Kathy Parrott's classroom.

Parrott's days are usually long. In her class before 8:00 a.m., she averages leaving at about 5:30 p.m., long after students have departed at about 2:45. She often works in her classroom on weekends, "where

18

it is so quiet and I can get a lot done." Even while not in the classroom, she can often be seen at sales rummaging through materials she can use to help boys and girls learn. "I can find deals for little or nothing," she said, "and I just hate to waste the school system's money. It's not that they won't buy me things—they have whenever I've really needed it." Parrott also has a private lawn care business she runs in the summer. "I need it to help buy things for the classroom," she said.

In the "roll up your sleeves and get to working" world of special education, Parrott is one of the true models. One may wonder what innate drive, what *invisible* force, drives a person to give so much of their own energy, endurance and, often, unconditional love—simply to make a positive difference in someone else's life.

"I guess I always see the underdog," she said. "It goes back to when I was little and I had a cousin with really severe disabilities. His name is Brian and he was not supposed to live past three years. He is now in his thirties and has lived a lot longer than anyone thought he would. I believe that everyone needs something to make them feel good about themselves, whether it be a job, playing an instrument or some other talent"

As if Parrott needs more work to do, she recently bought a full service trophy business located in Versailles. Her intent is, as usual, noble. The business is largely run by adults with disabilities and is quite unique for Kentucky. "I hope some day that the students in my class will work there," she said with anticipation.

LaBarbara describes Parrott as "something special. She's a great person and really cares. You can see by watching her in the class-room."

Parrott's students, as she loves, encourages and provides opportunities for them, perform way beyond most people's expectations—except Ms. Kathy's.

Jim Lyon, Sr.

Disabilities No Match for Judge Lyon

If anyone ever told Jim Lyon he couldn't be a high achiever while dealing with three limbs missing and one disfigured, he didn't listen.

In fact, not being successful was a thought very far from his thinking. His mother made sure of that years ago, soon after he was born in 1931. Her early encouragement helped propel Lyon to an illustrious career in law and politics, serving two terms in the Kentucky General Assembly, district and circuit court judgeships for Lewis and Greenup counties, and a long and prosperous law practice in his hometown of Raceland. "My mother used to say 'My baby doesn't have any hands and doesn't have any leg, but he has a mind,' and that always sat well with me," said Lyon, in his clear and deliberate voice. "I never dwell on the negatives."

Lyon was born with stubs instead of arms. That meant that the two limbs coming down from his shoulders did not quite reach the elbow area. The right leg, also a stub, did not reach the knee, plus his left foot was malformed. Despite those physical deformities, Lyon's childhood was remarkably similar to his peers who grew up in his Raceland neighborhood more than seventy years ago. Fitted with an artificial leg, Lyon ran and played softball and football with other children. He occasionally got in fights, often with his brother. That sort of thing did not particularly bother his mother, who wanted her son treated like everyone else. That included not enrolling him in a special school. She insisted that her son attend the regular schools in their local area.

Lyon did well academically, graduating from Raceland High School in 1949 within a few points of being class salutatorian. That following fall, he enrolled in pre-law classes at the University of Kentucky. There he found a lot of support from the administration and teachers, who were willing to make adjustments to help him navigate the rigors of his challenging classes.

Jim Lyon, Sr.

"I can't say enough good about UK. They took care of me and gave me a chance. I just had to do the work," Lyon said. Because of the unwieldy nature of using the hooks attached to his arm stubs, Lyon often was allowed the use of a scribe while taking exams. "The administration said that it was too much writing at once for me," he said.

Lyon proudly graduated with a law degree from UK in 1955, then set up his law practice in the town of Greenup, near Raceland. He worked hard and began to establish a growing client load, but only after making an adaptation relating to his disability. "I had a lot to do to compete with the other lawyers in town, and using my hooks to do paperwork slowed me down," he said, "so I quit using the hooks and I worked much faster." That change entailed Lyon to simply secure the writing instrument by bringing his two arm stubs together around it.

In 1958, Lyon executed a bold move, even for someone who did not deal with the challenge of physical disabilities. He ran for election to Kentucky's General Assembly, representing Greenup County. He won.

"I was interested in politics from day one and I had a chance to run for state representative," he said. The details of serving in Frankfort, though, made it a near daunting task for a young legislator. He was continually approached by lobbyists and colleagues to vote their way on issues. "There were times I'd be awakened by someone in the middle of the night about an issue. It got to be so demanding that I got boils on my arm stubs at times. I had legislative stress," he said with a grin.

Lyon held up well, though, and completed two, two-year terms from 1958 to 1962 while he continued his private law practice. In 1960, in the middle of his legislative service, Lyon got married. It has been a good fit for the two. His wife, Jean, has been his supportive partner, and much of the time she served as his secretary in his law office.

Though Lyon lost an election for county attorney in 1962, he served as circuit court master commissioner from 1962 to 1978, then as district judge into the '80s. On the day after Christmas in 1986, Lyon suffered a heart attack and recuperated at home for about six months after bypass surgery. He retired in 1994, with son, James, Jr., taking over his practice. The couple's other son, Benjamin, is a physician in Georgetown. Truly, the "good mind" that Jim Lyon's mother talked about was passed to the next generation.

Lyon has an obvious warmth and graciousness about him. His amiable way likely is a product of the love of many who have helped him along the way. He carries with him accumulated feelings of gratitude to his mother, his wife and children, the people in college who gave him a chance, his former colleagues and long-time friends.

Along the way, he has helped others. He remembers his days as judge in the courtroom, when he tried to mix mercy with justice.

"I always tried to give people who stood before me another chance. One man was guilty of a DUI and I went a little easy on him. I hoped he would do better. Years later, he told me that because of that chance, he turned his life around...quit drinking and got back with his wife," he said. Lyon also made it clear he didn't like to make pontificating speeches in court—that might humiliate someone. "Plus, you never know if someone might get back at you later," he said.

Lyon, even in his career days, involved himself with civic activities. Besides belonging to the Methodist faith, he's been an active member of the Raceland Lions Club and served in the local youth football and baseball leagues.

These days, Jim Lyon, Sr. keeps busy by occasionally helping out his lawyer son, keeping up with UK sports, and doing a little automobile cruising in a car adapted to handle his physical needs. "I drive around town a little," he said with a smile, "mostly to McDonald's and sometimes I'll pick up groceries at the store for the wife."

In a world that is demanding and competitive—even for the able-bodied—Jim Lyon has proved that accentuating the positives, developing an attitude of focus, and accepting the support of others can turn a person born with serious physical disabilities into a genuine world-beater.

Dzevad and Merima Kreso

Bosnian Refugees Add to Life of Bardstown

The couple lived a charmed life. Dzevad won renown as a member of both the Bosnian national soccer team and later as a professional player. Living in a place where a fledgling democracy had many economic challenges, Dzevad and Merima Kreso owned a popular and prosperous restaurant in a large city, one where a former Yugoslavian president had dined. The couple had three healthy and well-adjusted children, and the family was well-connected socially. It was, for the Kresos, a happy existence.

Then, the war came.

The Bosnian War, from 1992 to 1995, is often referred to as a civil war. Merima Kreso disagrees. "It was a criminal war," her strong voice asserted. "People were stealing houses. Soldiers were coming, stealing pictures and cash…taking everything you had."

Their restaurant in Bana Luka was taken from them. For a while, the Kresos remained in Bosnia, trying to hold on to the best life they could muster in a land they loved and were deeply rooted. In the end, they decided to seek a better life elsewhere, away from imminent danger and a place where, Dzevad said, "there was an opportunity to succeed if you were willing to work hard."

Through an international program to help refugees, the Kresos were given a choice of three countries to enter: Australia, Canada, or the United States. "We wanted to come to a place that didn't have a socialistic government, a place where we could work hard and move up. We chose the United States," Dzevad said.

Dzevad and Merima Kreso

An interesting thing happened in the process of the Kreso's change of locations. A Bardstown minister, Ken Thompson, become a bit of a personal angel to the Kresos. "He chose us out of a list of people to be sponsored by his church when we came," Merima said. "He talked with his congregation about us and today we still have a great friendship with him and the church."

On July 21, 1995, the Bosnian family arrived in Bardstown—a long distance away from the war-torn Balkan region of Europe. The Kresos were looking only for a little help to get them started while they oriented themselves to new, and much different, surroundings. They got it, as the family was placed in an apartment and treated warmly by both the church congregation and the Bardstown community. It was appreciated by the couple. "In the two months we arrived as refugees, these people gave us what we needed—and for life," Merima said.

Uplifted by the show of support, the couple began to master the English language and soon leased a downtown restaurant at 114 North Third St. The customers came—and they kept coming. The Kreso children, all girls and ages eight, twelve, and fourteen, became a part of the school system and did well in their classes. In time, Dzevad received the opportunity to share his gifted soccer skills as nearby St. Catharine College's soccer coach, and later at Bethlehem High School. Merima worked hard with Dzevad at the restaurant, often sixty to seventy hours per week. In short, the Nelson County community had gained five new members who worked hard and contributed.

The Kresos were now established transplants in another country, happy and admired by many who knew them. But there were more dreams to chase. Down the street from their restaurant, there were a couple of empty, adjacent buildings that had seen no life for more than thirty years. They were, at one time, the Arco and Melody movie theatres, formerly thriving entertainment centers in Bardstown. For Dzevad and Merima, memories of their dining establishment in Bosnia began to stir them. Could these remnants of another era, these almost forgotten representations of local history, be turned into something special for the Kresos—and something unique for the good people of Bardstown?

"Dzevad was afraid about it at first," Merima said, "but I really wanted to do it."

"I told her that if she really wanted to do it, we would," Dzevad added.

The decision was made. The Kresos would buy both buildings and renovate them into a large, exquisite restaurant and café. That is, if they could obtain a loan. "We were not able to get the loan from the first bank we tried," Dzevad said, "but the second bank did. They are very happy about it now."

After purchasing the real estate in 2002, what seemed an almost daunting project became an invigorating adventure that motivated them, according to their web site, "to preserve the original features of the structure as well as enabling themselves to suit the needs of the restaurant."

"We began to remove the many layers of flooring," Dzevad said. "It was hard work and we got down on our knees using a knife to clean

26

it. We found a treasure of terrazzo flooring there." The process of renovation took about two years. What's more impressive is that the Kresos continued to successfully operate the other restaurant during that period.

Today, Kreso's Family Restaurant and Mozart Café is one of the most popular fine dining establishments in the area. And it looks to be around for a while. "People from other cities have asked us about moving our business there, but we love it here," Merima said.

Mary Casey, a friend who renovated another building next door, praised the Kresos. "What remarkable people they are! Up early every morning, a full day at the restaurant, and more often than not their heads don't hit the pillow until after midnight. And they have been doing this since they have arrived in the U.S."

Betty Seay traveled with the Kresos a few years ago. They shared an emotional experience as they revisited the former restaurant. "Instead of feeling bitter about their financial loss, they have chosen to look at life in a positive view and count their blessings everyday. They are also loyal to friends and family and are very generous," she said. Speaking of loyalty, Dzevad's former soccer players at Bethlehem High, said colleague Tommy Reed, "always touch base with him when they pass through Bardstown. There is a tremendous bond between him and his players."

Mayor Dick Heaton has known the Kresos since they arrived in Bardstown. "They came here with nothing," he said, "and became a big part of our community." Heaton also talked about the cosmopolitan nature of the restaurant the Kresos have influenced. "I noticed one day that we had, sitting around my gathering, representatives from five different ethnic groups."

Hard work. Appreciation and gratitude. A creative and entrepreneurial spirit. In truth, Bosnia's loss has been a fabulous, inspiring gain for the people of Bardstown, and likewise for all Kentuckians.

Marie Braun

Advocating from a Wheelchair

Marie Braun learned long ago that life's playing field is not always level.

Born with quadrilplegic cerebral palsy in rural Sebastion Branch, in Breathitt County, more than fifty years ago, little Marie Louise Miller soon became a case for the child welfare system and was placed into the Frankfort State Hospital. It was an institution—a place, Braun said later, "where people put their children in this home because they thought that they were 'retarded' and could do nothing for themselves."

Marie hoped that she could find foster parents who would love her unconditionally, even though she had difficulty with bladder and weight control. As she grew older, she prayed for the day she could move out of the confines of the hospitals and nursing homes. Marie dreamed of a day when she would someday meet a soul mate and be intimate—both emotionally *and* physically. Mostly, she just wanted the chance to breathe the invigorating air of opportunity that she saw others enjoy everyday.

At least in part, her wishes came true. She now owns a battery-powered chair that works well when she hasn't overworked it. When she was about eight-years-old, she gained the parent and daughter-like love of an aging couple from Lexington, the late William and Pearl Ann Lowenthal. Then, with a life-changing and inspirational boost from her now deceased soul mate and husband, Bill Braun, Marie escaped institutional life and today lives in an apartment by herself in Covington. These personal advancements have, for Marie Braun, led to an insatiable desire to make life better for other persons who share similar challenges.

Marie Braun

She has become an effective advocate for the disabled. In the last twenty-five years, Braun has spoken publicly about such issues as the education of disabled children, personal attendant care for the disabled, Medicaid and employment issues. Besides being a persistent voice for change around Covington, Braun has carried her message to rallies and hearings in Frankfort and Washington, D.C. "Disabled people are human like everyone else," said Braun. "They have the same wants and desires and want acceptance in society."

It sometimes takes dramatic measures to show the able-bodied world that more needs to be done for the disabled. For example, she led the mayor of Covington, along with other officials, on a "wheelchair tour" of city streets, pointing out many wheelchair accessibility issues. "One of the commissioners fell out of a wheelchair," she said with a grin. As a result of Braun's proactive stance, positive changes were soon implemented on Covington's streets. Then there was the public transit system, and Braun's influence helped there, too. Her cerebral palsy makes voice articulation difficult, but it hasn't stopped Braun from being effective and expanding her advocacy skill levels by obtaining her GED. "Advocacy is long and hard work," she noted, "but sometimes it pays off. All the advocacy I have done throughout the years, whether it was in attending workshops, various meetings, or public hearings has helped me learn a lot about advocacy and how to go about it. Talking with and writing letters to my legislators, and writing letters to the newspaper editors and appearing on television and videos as an advocate hopefully have helped those in the community to learn to speak out for themselves and others."

Another long-time community activist in Covington, Bennie Doggett, is impressed with Braun. "At city government meetings, I've seen her wheel her chair right up to the faces of the officials," she said with a laugh. "That woman is beautiful inside."

Her spirited desire to do something for others might have lain dormant if not for Bill Braun. She met him in 1977 at Ridgeview Nursing Home in Covington, and against the advice of others, they were married in 1980. With the urging of Bill, who had formerly been labeled "mildly retarded," they left Ridgeview to start an independent life in the Covington community. Bill's recurring message to Marie, "you have rights and you need to fight for them," soon was indelibly written in her psyche. She gradually began to throw off the fear of facing the outside world. The sight of Marie in her wheelchair and Bill pushing her along Covington's streets became a common occurrence. Besides going about their daily living activities, the couple found themselves involved in proactive ventures to help others with disabilities. David Wecker wrote in a March 1, 2004 *Kentucky Post* column: "They signed up for committees. They were elected to boards. They wrote letters to their congressmen, their state rep, the mayor. They found out where various resources were, and they used them. Marie says she was an advocate before she knew she was an advocate."

Bill Braun died in 1994. Marie still grieves, but pushes onward in speaking out for her rights and the rights of the disabled population. Close friend Vickie Cimprich, who met Marie over thirty-five years ago, called her "the consummate extrovert." Marie has an active membership in the Covington Human Rights Commission, the Disability Coalition of Northern Kentucky and has been the chairman of the Kentucky Developmental Disabilities Council.

Currently, besides her volunteer work, Marie works part time for The Salvation Army. She sits by the "kettle" and rings the bell proudly and sells the magazine of inspiration called *The War Cry*. She talks to all who listen about the rights of the disabled. She tells people bits and pieces of her own story. Some day, she hopes to publish her ninety-six-page manuscript about her life, called *Any Way: My Stories of Advancement and Advocacy*. Transcribed by Vickie Cimprich, Marie Braun tells of her difficult childhood, those who uplifted her and those who encouraged her. She relates in authentic detail her failures, her successes, her hopes and dreams. Her message can be summed up in a few "don't" phrases. "Don't let people tell you you can't do it. Don't be afraid to follow your dreams."

In 2007 she accepted a position as Disabilities Rights Trainer with the Kentucky Office of Protection and Advocacy.

Don Rose

Helping Veterans Tell Their Stories

It bothered Don Rose a whole lot when he heard that American military veterans are dying off at a rate of about 1,500 per day. It also bothered him that with the loss of so many of our veterans, an uncountable multitude of personal accounts of war's cruelty and human pathos, as well as stirring stories of individual bravery and sacrifice, would forever go untold—in effect, deleted from history.

The fact that many of his very closest friends were ones faithful in service to their country also helped fire his juices. Accordingly, the Korean War-era Marine reacted pretty much the way he always has when he sees a serious human need—he decided to do what he could to make things better, and immediately made a plan to implement it.

Rose, working through the sponsorship of the Library of Congress Veterans History Project, the American Folklife Association and the national AARP organization, began interviewing scores of Kentucky's oldest military veterans. Since 2003, a total of 120 interviews have been archived. With the assistance of friend Richard Doughty, the two patriots from Winchester have meticulously chronicled the sometimes gut-wrenching but always from-the-heart stories, of Americans who fought in defense of freedom in all parts of the world.

The audio and video taped sessions are being placed in two places. At the Clark County Public Library, tapes can be checked out or viewed on site. The Morehead State University History Department is also a beneficiary of Rose's efforts.

Clark Library director Julie Maruskin is impressed by Rose's leadership in the project. "The Library of Congress has collected 25,000 interviews from all fifty states over a period from 2000-2005," she said. "So Don has collected nearly half of one percent of the total interviews received from thousands of volunteers nationwide." Maruskin estimates the time expended per interview involves "as much as thirty-five hours, including preparation, actual interviews, documentation and delivery of all documents to our library and the Library of Congress...truly astonishing."

Don Rose

At Morehead State, history department chairman Dr. Yvonne Baldwin is grateful for Rose's work. "I was amazed at his (Rose's) dedication to the cause, but also by his demeanor. He simply wants the stories told and wants them to be accessible for future generations." Baldwin leads a project called Connecting the Generations, and Rose brought a veteran group to share at the university. "It was one of the most moving interactions I have ever witnessed," she said.

Though small amounts of money are occasionally donated to help Rose defray costs, the financial sacrifice is something he's willing to absorb—a price, he thinks, that's much less than what most of his interviewees have paid. Rose reports the oral accounts of veterans who have lost limbs, lost buddies and who still suffer the effects from war. "I know pretty well the questions I need to ask," he said, "and I let the veterans do most of the talking."

One point has been made clear to Rose through the process—with the exception of World War II, most veterans wonder about the need for the U.S. to have been in any war since 1941. "In particular, the Viet

Nam War looks to be the most unpopular among those I've interviewed. Many from that war were treated very badly when they returned home."

Rose is quick to state his own view on war. "In my opinion, war is the worst possible way to solve any disagreement. They just ought to let the leaders of two countries fight it out and save all the trouble for everyone else," he stated, maybe only somewhat facetiously.

Winchester Mayor Ed Burtner, a Marine veteran, said Rose is "doggedly determined and at the forefront to see that our veterans' oral histories are recorded. He is a tremendous asset to our community."

Despite the time-consuming, often exhausting work, Rose has no plans to retire from the project. "As long as I have names given to me, I will continue to interview," said Rose. His words are said with a sense of assurance, even though Rose has recently been doing battle with prostrate cancer, and he has had to curtail some of his work.

Rose won the Andrus Award for Community Service, the highest recognition of Kentucky's AARP state chapter, in 2006. He was also honored by a special "Don Rose Day" in the city of Winchester. And though the veterans project is what most people connect Rose's involvement, he participates in other significant ways to help people. In 2005, for example, he and his wife Janet taught seven "Defensive Driving Classes" for the local AARP. The couple, working closely together, spent an average of twelve hours per class, including preparation, transportation and teaching. It's not unusual for Rose to be seen driving senior citizens to important appointments, such as meetings in Frankfort regarding AARP issues. Rose and his wife are currently working to start local AARP chapters in other central Kentucky towns. He also serves faithfully on the Honor Guard as a member of the Marine Corps League in Winchester. And Rose's vegetable garden provides generously for elderly neighbors. Whatever it takes, it seems, is what he'll do when he knows of another in need.

It still bothers Rose that veterans are dying off before they have a chance to tell their stories. He knows that despite his best efforts and those of others, some experiences will go to the grave, untold. But for

Rose, it won't be because he didn't do his part. Baldwin may have best summed up Rose's contribution. "Don Rose is a hero. Professional historians and researchers are indebted to those who are willing to share their life experiences in such a meaningful and endearing format, and without Don Rose, that opportunity (for many American military veterans) would likely have been missed."

CONTACT INFORMATION:
Veterans History Project
Library of Congress / American Folklife Center
101 Independence Avenue S.E.
Washington, D.C. 20540-4615
Web site http://www.loc.gov/folklife/vets/

Patrick Henry and Patrick John Hughes

Inspiring Father-Son Partnership 'Rolls' Past Disabilities

Patrick John Hughes had high aspirations for his first and new-born son, Patrick Henry. He couldn't wait to watch young Patrick show grit, to be a true gentleman. Dad even hoped that his boy might grow to be a successful and popular musician, or possibly a sports star featured on ESPN.

Two decades later, Dad's dreams were realized in grand style and with overflowing acclamation—but not like he had first imagined. Patrick Henry and Patrick John Hughes were the subjects of national TV and news coverage for the inspiring story of being a part of the University of Louisville's marching band, with Dad proudly pushing his wheelchair-bound, blind, student son around the football field as Patrick played the trumpet.

Continually, Patrick repeated to the media some version of "Big deal, I'm blind, but God gave me the ability to play the trumpet and the piano." He modeled, by attitude and actions, that a person who can't see and can't walk can nevertheless play beautiful music, can make high grades in class, and perhaps most importantly, can be a well-adjusted and happy individual who can move people to rise above their own challenges.

Patrick became the first ever non-athlete to win the Disney Wide World of Sports Spirit Award, announced on ESPN at the Orange Bowl. He was profiled in *People* magazine, *USA Today*, *Sports Illustrated* and numerous other print media. He was featured on "Good

Morning America" and on the "Oprah Winfrey Show." He began getting invitations to speak and display his accomplished music skills. He appeared on numerous radio talk shows.

Patrick, with typical clear and articulate speech, downplayed all the attention. "I don't care about all that attention I'm getting," he said. "It's just that it's fun and I enjoy meeting new people. God has just given me the ability to use my music to inspire others."

What brought the two to such unexpected national acclaim was a long and circuitous path that started in 1987, when Patrick was born.

Patrick's arrival into the world brought disappointment for both parents after he was diagnosed with a rare genetic disorder that left him, literally, with no eyes and the added burden of an inability to straighten his arms and legs.

"We had played by all the rules. Patricia had a good pregnancy. There was no drugs or alcohol or anything. We wondered why it happened to us," Dad explained.

After a short time of "feeling sorry for ourselves," the couple began dealing with how they best could help their son. The father saw something special about Patrick in the first few months of infancy, while he was doing what babies do—namely, screaming.

"I laid him on the piano and played notes to him," said the elder Hughes, "and, like a switch, Patrick got quiet immediately." By the time the child was nine-months old, he sat at the piano in a high chair, not "banging" the keys with his thick fingers, but noticeably reacting to the differences in the key sounds as he touched them.

"I could see the wheels turning as he would hit a note," said Hughes, "and then he'd, by trial and error, play them back to me as I'd call them out." By age two, Patrick was playing requests, such as "You are My Sunshine" and "Twinkle, Twinkle Little Star." He was becoming the darling of Patrick John and Patricia Hughes, as well as others who knew the family.

Patrick Henry and Patrick John Hughes

With what the elder Hughes called "phenomenal" support from the Jefferson County Public Schools, Patrick was successfully mainstreamed into regular classes from kindergarten through high school. He received Braille-system training early and it became an integral part of his learning. His grades were consistently nearly all A's, and in Atherton High School, Patrick made the Kentucky all-state teams in both chorus and band.

Patrick grins when he tells how his music teachers used him as a model to motivate other students. "The teachers would say 'Patrick is memorizing his music, so if he can do it, you can do it'"

Dad cited the numerous teachers who helped his son with daily adaptations in the classroom as a large part of his success. With more than a hint of fatherly pride, Dad remarked that "the special needs teachers were always fighting to get Patrick in their classes because of his attitude and work habits," Hughes said. "He was a good student."

In the summer of 2006, Patrick enrolled as a freshman in the University of Louisville. He would take full advantage of U of L's resources for helping students with disabilities to succeed, but his father would play a huge role, too. Dad would work at UPS at nights in order to wheel his son around campus every school day and assist him in the classroom. Long nights and short mornings of rest, and long days supporting a very appreciative son.

Not surprisingly, Patrick had a strong desire to play his trumpet in the Louisville pep band at basketball games. There was a problem, however. A school rule stated that, in order to be a member of the pep band, a student was also required to be a part of the marching band—apparently not a possibility for the wheelchair-bound freshman.

A door opened, however, for what Patrick always ever needed anyway—a simple opportunity to shine. In a remarkable gesture of creativity and generosity, the marching band director, Greg Byrne, made a surprising proposal to Patrick. How about joining the marching band? And not just sit on the sideline playing, as he did in high school, but in formation, moving along with the other marchers. He would then be in compliance with the school rule and could later play in the pep band at basketball games.

Successful participation in the marching band would simply be a matter of logistics, and Dad was the key. He would be the power behind Patrick's wheelchair. Dad would have to practice and learn the formations and drills like all the other band members. The challenge would be enormous, but both Patrick and his father were game to the idea.

It started in band summer camp, with twelve-hour days. There was heat, a heavy wheelchair and his 165-pound son aboard. There were stops, starts, and plenty of do-overs. Sometimes there were collisions, too.

But it worked, and the summer-camp experience prepared them for the season to start, with three practices a week plus a game, usually on Saturday. It would also make Dad's already tough days with Patrick in the college classroom seem a little easier, but still challenging.

"The first two weeks of class were brutal," said Dad. "Placing special orders for text books on CD's, for example, and having to wait for them to arrive." In the meantime, Dad read Patrick's text assignments to him until the materials came. In a twenty-four-hour world, this father needed about twice that many.

"There wasn't much time to sleep, but it's what a father is supposed to do. I didn't have much time to pity myself," said Dad. "I was blessed when I thought about being better off than ninety per cent of the world's population."

As the marching-performance season got going, along with Louisville's highly successful football Cardinals, attention for the inspiring story of the Hughes' twosome came quickly. It made people feel good, and it made people think about rich possibilities in their own lives—and it was noticed throughout the world.

"Even today, we get emails everyday from all around the country, even other countries like Indonesia and South Africa telling us what this has meant to them," said Dad. "We see that there is a reason for all that has happened to us. We were only occasional churchgoers, though believers, when Patricia and I got married, but when Patrick came along it changed all that."

Patrick has accepted the faith of his parents. "Oh, yeah. Our faith is very important to us. We go to church every chance we get, including when we're out of town we find a church to attend," he said. "I am also using Rick Warren's program of reading through the Bible in a year." Then he smiled broadly as he noted, "I always say grace, even when I just take a drink of water."

Along with Patrick's school and band activities, the invitations to speak and play music at churches, conferences and other venues are keeping the family busy—almost too busy. "We do the best we can, because we really like to travel, but it's getting a bit hard to handle all of them," said Dad.

The Hughes family includes two other boys, Cameron and Jesse. "I am very proud of them, too," said Dad. "They do well in school and with their activities. And, they seem to handle Patrick's acclaim very well. I want to support them, also."

Largely as a result of the outpouring of appreciation for the inspirational nature of the story, the Hughes family was selected by TV's "Extreme Makeover: Home Edition" to move into a newly built home. They were cheered on by a large crowd and the adoration of the city of Louisville, and the family's house has been designed to allow Patrick more accessible living Coinciding with the development, Patrick and his father will be honored by their likenesses on a downtown mural.

Through their partnership, Patrick John and Patrick Henry Hughes have learned from each other some valuable life lessons.

"Dad taught me that it doesn't matter what kind of disability you have, you can't expect to get sympathy," Patrick Henry said. "He let me know that if you set your mind to something, you can do it."

"Patrick has taught me to never say never in whatever happens," Dad said.

Looking into the future, after the last marching band performance on wheels takes place and the last class in college is taken, can we expect these two models of the best in human spirit to continue their close working relationship?

"That depends on Patrick," said Dad. "He'll be getting older and probably more independent.

"But if he needs me, I'll be there."

Dr. John Belanger

The Good Physician of Paint Lick

John Belanger has a kind heart intermingled with a super-sized portion of idealism.

When he was a small boy, he had his dreamy eyes wide open when his family took those long, leisurely drives from their home in Louisville to diverse parts of Kentucky. "I remember going through a small town in eastern Kentucky and seeing a billboard with the words 'WE NEED A DENTIST.' I thought then how good it would be someday for me to go to a place where I was really needed. It was a vision I kept with me," explained the soft-spoken Berea resident.

Belanger, one of nine children, later chose medicine rather than dentistry as his career choice. His desire to land where he was "really needed," however, became a reality. Dr. John Belanger today serves twenty to thirty patients a day and has seen over 7500 individuals come into his office since he opened the Paint Lick Family Clinic, an "affordable care" medical service that is open to all, in Garrard County. The practice opened in 2000, and it is fair to say it has thrived from the beginning—just like Belanger envisioned.

It took awhile for the dream job to come, however. Belanger was a member of the Community Health Center medical staff near Berea for eleven years. While there, he got a little of what he wanted, a non-profit medical practice that catered to those of modest financial means. There were some things that bothered him, though. "We received federal funding," Belanger said, "and that made for more restrictions.

As we got larger, administrative things got in the way of serving people. I guess I'm a simple person who just wants to take care of individuals, and I found myself getting very frustrated." Belanger admitted that he started to obsess about making a change, and, "was getting a bit irritable" at home, too. That added impetus for him and his wife, Sarah, to begin an earnest search for a practice more in line with his ideals—one that served anyone, even those with no insurance and little resources to pay—and with few strings attached.

Dr. John Belanger

Out for a weekend drive in the country, the couple crossed a small bridge over a creek, then looked to the left. *There's the building,* John thought, *the one in my mind's eye.* The bridge they crossed, over Paint Lick Creek, led them from Madison County into the small town of Paint Lick. The red brick and rustic building sat in a row of several connected structures with the post office farthest from the creek. The First Southern Bank dominated another grouping of buildings across the street. Paint Lick was a quaint, quiet, but alive town, and John and Sarah felt like they had been dropped into the place they had been looking to find, or, at least, had taken the first step toward that wish.

Now possessing a spirit of anticipation, Belanger began talking to people around Paint Lick, expressing his desire to open a medical clinic. Within a week, he was led to Dean Cornett. Cornett was a local community activist, a Mother Theresa-like individual who had spun a network of small-town, charitable links which resulted in two things— people's needs being communicated and, more importantly, people's needs met. She carried out her acts of community assistance plus lived in the red brick building under the auspices of The Friends of Paint Lick.

After Cornett's husband died, she had forthrightly dedicated herself to service to others and reliance on God to meet her worldly needs. Belanger recounted his first meeting with the tiny lady who was fighting advanced Parkinson's disease. "She met me at the door and told me she had been praying for a doctor. I told her that I was the doctor she was praying for. We discussed the possibility of using part of the Friends building, but decided on something different," he said. "She walked us around and showed us the old garage next to the Friends building." A sort of providential certitude colored Dean Cornett's next remarks. "I want this garage to be a doctor's office. I'll give you the building and want you to be using it within a year."

So there, in 1999, Dr. Belanger had the setting for his dream to come true. There was much to do and much to overcome. Numerous questions needed answering. What kind of renovating would the garage need? How would a staff be assembled, and how many? What about the financial considerations of running such an endeavor? Would the community support the project?

Though Belanger, like Cornett, felt "God's inspiration" working in the series of events, he admitted he became a little nervous as he "started looking at the nuts and bolts." He would be leaving a $90,000 per year salary with health insurance and retirement benefits. He would be entering, humanly speaking, uncharted financial waters. But his mission carried a wealth of positives. Belanger's wife's enthusiasm, the Cornett's inspiration, and the fact that "no one of my parents or eight siblings told me I was crazy" emboldened him. He was ready to do it.

Cornett's Friends of Paint Lick, plus Belanger's well-wishers, began to move. In 10 months, $200,000 was raised. That included a $30,000 check from Bill Diehl, a service-minded man Belanger met at an award dinner recognition at Defiance College in Ohio. A tip about a devout building contractor who was between jobs—given to Belanger at a Richmond church service—resulted in important assistance in tearing down the garage and replacing it with what would become a physician's office. Construction started in June 2000, and was ready by mid-September. There *would* be a Paint Lick Family Clinic in the small, rural town, and Dr. John Belanger was even an important part of the manual work force. "I had some time after resigning from the Community Health Center," said Belanger, "and I became a laborer along with the others for a few months. I really enjoyed doing it."

An attempt to keep overhead low for the operation of the clinic has paid off. Belanger's small, but efficient and loyal staff is filling a genuine need for the people in the Paint Lick area. He has an office manager, one full-time and another half-time certified medical assistant. Several volunteers help immeasurably with finding inexpensive, or even free, medications that usually are dispensed from the office. Belanger has attributed himself a $35,000 per year salary—small in comparison to general practitioners across the nation. He has made a point to pay his staff better than average, "so the gap between my pay and theirs is not as much as it usually is." Anyone is welcome to come for treatment, and Belanger attempts to spend twenty minutes with each person. Patients are charged $25 for the first office visit, $20 thereafter, and the clinic is open four days a week for a total of forty hours. Payment, if necessary, can be postponed, but inability to pay does not disallow medical treatment. The clinic does not handle insurance claims other than Medicaid. "I like to keep things simple," Belanger is fond of saying.

Belanger finds satisfaction as he thinks about the typical cross-section of patients who daily sit in the Paint Lick Clinic waiting room. "There are educated and non-educated, some have financial recourses and some don't. It doesn't matter to us."

Asked about his personal dreams for the future, Belanger replied in his soft, humble manner. "I do hope to be some sort of a positive influence, to do more to educate the world about the plight of the uninsured. We hope to remain flexible here at the clinic so we can make changes quickly." Belanger also praised his personal heroes who have shaped his life, people such as dedicated physician colleagues,

Dean Cornett and people at his church. "These have always been the type of people I've looked up to, who are just ordinary people who do amazing things."

Out there, no doubt, are people who hold Dr. John Belanger in the same regard.

For those interested in supporting the work of the Paint Lick Family Clinic, contact 859-925-2444 or P.O. Box 65, Paint Lick, KY 40461.

Jamie Vaught

Sports Passion Helps Beat Hearing Limitations

Jamie Vaught, for as long as he can remember, has been "crazy about the Cats." So much so, he has written four books about those Cats, who are better known to non-Kentuckians as the University of Kentucky Wildcats basketball program.

The love of his favorite team, along with sports in general, may be the biggest reason why Vaught, who doctors correctly labeled as "severely hard of hearing" as a small child, has overcome his physical barrier to become a successful author, columnist and college professor.

Born in 1956 in Somerset two months prematurely, his parents quickly realized that little Jamie had something that wasn't normal. "When I was about two, my parents said I was real grouchy, fussy and did not respond to talking," said Vaught from his office at the Southeast Kentucky Community and Technical College, in Middlesboro.

After the diagnosis became known, the family established a plan for young Jamie. Part of the plan was to decide where Jamie would go to school. Danville's School for the Deaf was considered, but one of the state's smallest school systems at that time, Science Hill, near Somerset, offered to work closely with the family to help with Jamie's special needs. That would allow for him to stay close to home.

"I became the family project," said Vaught with a grin, "and my mother and grandmother would work with me almost every night. My sister was sixteen years older and got married at eighteen, so she couldn't help."

48

With the support of his family, his natural intelligence and a good work ethic, Vaught became an academic high achiever—all the way through his bachelor's and master's degrees at the University of Kentucky.

His academic success was not predicted by some. "The doctors told my mother that I would always be in the bottom third of my classes but I was in the top third," Vaught said. It didn't come easy, especially in college. "I had note-takers, some good, [and] some bad. There were also some teachers who had a beard, which made it

Jamie Vaught

hard to lip read." He finished college with a 3.2 grade point average in his major of accounting—a major, incidentally, that was recommended to him because "they said I wouldn't have to be around other people very much."

While taking only a few journalism courses, Vaught joined UK's school newspaper, the *Kentucky Kernal*. He became the sports editor and could now report on the Wildcats. He was in blue heaven and he knew it, but it only prepared him for what was to come in 1981—a position as a columnist for Oscar Combs's *Cats' Pause* weekly, a publication many UK fans consider almost of holy writ in importance. Vaught worked at the *Cats' Pause* for thirteen years, honing his writing craft and deepening his basketball knowledge—and his line of contacts—for a future book about Kentucky Wildcats basketball.

When *Crazy about the Cats* was in the research and writing stage, he did not have a publisher. "People told me it would be no trouble because of the interest in UK basketball, but it took awhile," he said. "I always knew I could use the interviews for my columns if I couldn't find a publisher."

Vaught's patience paid off. He finally hooked up with McClanahan Publishing, in Kuttawa, Kentucky. The book, a series of profiles of former UK players, or those around the program, was published in 1991. It was a hit, selling about 11,000 copies.

In describing the extra difficulty of producing his books, Vaught said, "I get someone to help me transcribe the tapes, often my mother. I double-check anything said that is controversial. Sometimes, people I talk to get a little impatient with me when I have to ask them to repeat what they said. I just say, 'Excuse me, I'm hard of hearing and I need to lip read.' Most are really nice about it, though." Also, Vaught's disability makes it impractical to interview by phone, necessitating all of them to be conducted in person. "Having email today," pointed out Vaught, "makes things a lot easier. I can't misquote anybody that way."

Dick Gabriel, long-time TV and radio reporter on UK sports, said Vaught is "…passionate about sports, and a very good writer. He's been able to successfully combine the two as a freelance writer. He also happens to be hearing-impaired. And I say 'happens' because it's never seemed to hinder him when it comes to interviewing athletes and writing about them. He reads lips so well that I've seen the reactions of folks who were surprised to learn he has a hearing problem."

Besides the Wildcats, Vaught loves to tell about his relationship with one of the great major league baseball players of all-time, Roberto Clemente. It started in the 1960s on a trip to Crosley Field, in Cincinnati, where ten-year-old Vaught and his father went to see the Reds and Pirates play. "I was standing in the back of a crowd with my father in a Cincinnati hotel lobby," Vaught explained, "and Roberto Clemente walked through. I had sent him a letter a while before that time. With everybody around him, he looked to the back of the crowd and saw me and told *me* to come to the front. I walked up and passed by the other fans."

What came next will always stick in Vaught's memory.

"I asked Clemente if he got the letter I sent to him. He didn't know, but he said he'd check. One week later, I received a bunch of stuff in the mail from him. He did check," Vaught said proudly. Later, the young hard-of-hearing boy received an autographed bat from the Hall of Famer, and he was also mentioned in several of Clemente's biographies, dramatizing the ballplayer's generosity and well known sense of concern for others.

Today, Jamie Vaught is a professor of business administration and accounting at Southeast Kentucky Community and Technical College. He had previously taught at Kentucky schools St. Catharine College and Sue Bennett College. Despite his physical disability, his personal and professional achievements are the envy of many.

Rose Ellen Allen

Helping the Infirmed

There likely will come a time, if not *already* experienced, when each of us may find ourselves spending a significant amount of time tending to another's needs. The most obvious time, for many, is while taking care of small children. Providing a lifeline for aging parents or helping a handicapped sibling are other examples. There are lots more. Though undertaken, typically, with loving intentions, the act of care-giving can be tough, can drain energy, and often pushes the limits of patience and perseverance. Few jump at the opportunity, some even resent it

Once in a while someone comes along who, unwittingly or not, ex-emplifies what true human care-giving is. Get to know Rose Ellen Allen, of Louisville.

The people who know her call her "Saint Rosie." She is in her sev-enties. They've watched her in action, continually, as she responded to her loved ones who were failing in their health and unable to live independently. Preparing special foods, providing a listening ear, helping with bathroom needs, tending to important paperwork mat-ters—these are just a few. Allen has been a Godsend of compassion for more than twenty-five years.

Her life as a care-giver began in earnest in the late 1970s, when Allen's seventeen-year-old Karla, second of five children, began to "limp and drag her feet," said Allen. Examined by a doctor, the condi-tion was termed a lower neuron motor disorder and Karla was given an exercise routine to do at home. "I thought the exercise actually made it worse but Karla was able to go on to St. Catharine College for a year," Allen said. In the aftermath, Karla lost her ability to walk. Still a gritty person, she enrolled in hometown Louisville's Sullivan College, where she courageously made her trips across campus in a wheelchair and the help of an aide. While Allen did her best to keep Karla's spirits positive, a new, formidable challenge arose. Karla's brother, Freddy, eighteen months younger, experienced the onset of

Rose Ellen Allen

similar symptoms. Though doctors at first didn't diagnose Freddy's condition as the same as his sister's, it soon became clear that it was.

Both Karla and Freddy made good efforts to take on normal responsibilities of an adult, daily work life. "She got her degree from Sullivan, but because of her limitations, Karla couldn't get a job," Allen said. "With some help from a person she knew, she became a volunteer aide at the Binet School for the Perceptually Handicapped, a position she loved." Freddy, not as academically oriented, decided not to go to college and worked an assortment of jobs. His physical problems continued, though, and his last attempt at employment ended at a sheltered workshop. Both siblings lost their ability to be mobile and became homebound. At that point, and for all concerned, life took a drastically different and tougher direction for Rose Ellen Allen and two of her children.

With the help of her husband, Fred, plus another lady outside the family, Allen became a nearly full-time care-giver in their home. Allen's training as a nurse was helpful, but the physical wear on her body after several years began to make the experience nearly unbearable. "The two kids had gained weight from having very little exercise and it became harder to lift them," she said. Concerned about her own health and her ability to serve her son and daughter, she struggled with some serious decisions about Karla and Freddy's future care.

Finally, after nearly two decades of daily care giving in her home, Allen began looking for a nursing home to help better serve the needs of her two children. She found a good one, though it was over twenty miles away, in Oldham County. The decision to put the care of her children into someone else's hands was difficult. There were mixed emotions. "It was just getting to be too much," Allen said tenderly, "and it was so very hard to do. They didn't want to go, but after being there for a short while, they started to like it better. I had been told that the younger employees and nursing assistants would gravitate toward Carla and Freddy, and it was true."

Allen continued her regimen of ministering to her young. She made the trip to Friendship Manor, in Pewee Valley, on Tuesdays and Thursdays. On Saturdays and Sundays, she arrived at the nursing home with home-cooked food—pureed for Karla because she had difficulty swallowing. In 1997, Rose Ellen arranged for her ninety-two-year-old mother from Bowling Green to join Karla and Freddy in residence at Friendship Manor. Though now caregiving for three, Allen remembers the positives. "Having Mother here instead of Bowling Green made things easier," Allen said. "Karla and Freddy were glad, too. They all loved my mother at the nursing home because she always told funny stories."

Though stringent as the time-consuming routine was, Allen's com-passionate nature and acceptance of her responsibility carried her forward, week by week, meal by meal, soothing word by soothing word. It was a test that many people younger than Allen would have failed. Then, as if not enough strain was leveled on one human being, her husband Fred received a grave medical diagnosis in August of 1999. He had pancreatic cancer. Soon afterward, he also suffered a debilitating stroke. He would need to be administered intense care by his wife in their home as she also kept her regular visits to Friendship Manor. Saint Rosie would answer the call again.

Allen doesn't see herself as a martyr—far from it. "I don't feel like any kind of hero. You just try to handle whatever is given you," she said. "I've had a lot of help through all of this." She talked about the lady who came to her house for nine years to help care for Karla and Freddy, her three other children and relatives, her friends and church members, and her God. "I always prayed a lot," she said, "and I would go to bed at night and ask God to take my burdens while I got some rest. Then I told Him I'd take them back the next day."

Her husband died in April 1999. Her mother lived to almost 101, dying in 2005. Daughter Karla died in June of 2006. Allen continues her regular trips to Friendship Manor, and is encouraged by Freddy's spirit. "He's doing fairly well," she said.

When asked what advice she might have for those who are called to be care givers, Allen mentioned several things besides her staple of prayer. "I always say to count your blessings, to name five things you can be thankful for every day. It's good to take little trips, and it's so important to take one day at a time," she said.

Rose Ellen Allen represents the best attributes of the human spirit. She has felt the pain and sadness of loss, yet continued steadfastly in her duty. She's experienced weariness, both physical and mental, yet never quit. She has acknowledged, by her actions, the inherent dignity of Karla, Freddy, her mother and her husband, leaving each with a sense of being loved. She has deepened the lives of those who have watched her. A neighbor and friend, Judy Egerton, said this of her. "To know her is to love and admire her. She is a role model and gentle superhero who makes the world a better place every day."

Few who know her would disagree.

Craig Williams

Viet Nam Vet Now Fights Environmental War

New York native Craig Williams had an understanding with his father while he was growing up. "My dad would punish me if I did something wrong, but if I didn't tell the truth about it, my punishment was far worse. He instilled in me the importance of always being truthful," he said.

Williams, who lives in Berea, now devotes his life to holding the American government and military to the same standard.

Though seeking, and telling, the truth has put Williams in some tough predicaments in his life, it has also resulted in safer existences for literally thousands of citizens who live near the U.S. government's various chemical weapons sites spread across the nation. Williams, along with his relatively small band of like-minded environmentalists, have courageously confronted U.S. military and government officials with meticulously researched and accurate information that demand compelling answers. His leadership has brought about significant policy changes, starting with the government's decision to find a safer way to dispose of chemical weapons than by incineration. After a long and tenacious battle, it happened at four of eight sites, including the Blue Grass Depot at Richmond.

Williams is best known for his efforts with safe disposal of chemical weapons, but his "truth" battles with the U.S. military began during his two-year hitch in the Army, when he was part of the Viet Nam era's "biggest draft in history" in 1968. He didn't start out with a political agenda. "I was like other kids, interested in consuming, clothes and things. I was not engaged about the war either way," he said.

Williams soon became part of the military police, and he also received intense training in the Vietnamese language. Both of those influences were critical to his future way of dealing with the world. He was part of an investigation team that looked at evidence of possible criminal actions of some officers at West Point. Williams believes that there was a bit of cover-up involved. "We

Craig Williams

found some guilt, and, as part of the agreement, the officers were sent elsewhere along with us."

For Williams, that meant being shipped unceremoniously to the jungles of Viet Nam, where he was assigned duty as an interrogator around which he again raised issues regarding the treatment of POWs. The charges he leveled led to his being reassigned "way out in nowhere guarding an ammunition outpost amongst some Vietnamese villages."

Williams was stung and disillusioned by the actions of the Army in the criminal investigation, and he began to evolve in another way. "In getting to know the Vietnamese people, I developed a better understanding of their perspective on the war and an appreciation of their culture," he said. "They wanted to determine their future themselves, and for years they were being invaded by other countries."

After his two-year time in the Army ended, Williams embraced his newfound mindset: that a flawed and untruthful leaning American military was involved in an unjust war. He helped organize Vietnam Veterans against the War, and his passionate desire to right wrongs and make life better for others was revved up. He participated in war protests all around the nation. In the anti-war crusade, he was introduced to future presidential candidate John Kerry who, Williams said, "served admirably in the War, but always had political aspirations, too."

The Viet Nam War ended in 1975, and Craig Williams had to figure out a new purpose in life after seven years of immersion in the international conflict. He lived for a while with friends in San Diego, and then moved with them to a rural area of Kentucky, near Elizabethtown, where the group lived somewhat hippie-style, raising vegetables and playing rock music. Soon, though, the group dwindled and Williams moved to tiny, and rural, Morrill, near Berea, and lived in a small cabin with no electricity.

"I was still adjusting to this culture after the Viet Nam experience," he said. There, he grew vegetables and attended classes at Eastern Kentucky University in Richmond, driving there "in my old pickup truck." He graduated with a degree in philosophy in 1978. Over the next few years, Williams married and gained an "instant family," attended The University of Kentucky Law School for a year, and had his own woodworking business. He co-founded the Viet Nam Veterans of America Foundation, Inc., an organization that eventually, in 1997, was a co-recipient of the 1997 Nobel Prize for its campaign to ban landmines.

Although Williams had a lot on his plate, he added something else. Williams got word of a public meeting regarding Richmond's Bluegrass Army Depot and its plan to destroy chemical weapons by using an incineration process. He made it a point to be there.

Williams took an immediate, cynical interest in the Army's plan to dispose of chemical weapons. Williams didn't question the fact that the Army wished to get rid of the chemical weapons, but only its method—by incineration. He began to study the issue intensely and found others around him with like concerns.

In 1990, Williams helped found the Kentucky Environmental Foundation, and under its umbrella, the Chemical Weapons Working Group (CWWG). The CWWG's immediate goal was to challenge three of the Army's premises regarding waste incineration. "We challenged their assertions that incineration was the only way to get rid of the wastes, that it was a safe way, and that once the decision was made, there was no way to turn it around," said Williams. It would prove to be a long, arduous battle, with Williams often working late into the night and begging for the patience of his own family members.

The CWWG became more and more visible, and working from Williams's home, then later from an office in Berea, money was raised to hire engineers and experts to produce a report to refute the public pronouncements from the Army. With the help of Kentucky politicians such as Representative Hopkins, Senators Ford and McConnell, along with the persistent efforts of Craig Williams and the CWWG, congressional hearings were held and each of the three Army arguments mentioned earlier were successfully challenged.

Williams's group supplied resources and information to other communities around the country facing similar challenges with the disposal of dangerous chemical weapons of mass destruction. A huge success came about in 1996 when the Army announced it would use a safer, water-based process for chemical disposal in Maryland and Indiana, and would suspend funds for incinerators in Colorado and Kentucky. That meant four of eight sites became imminently safer because of the CWWG's advocacy. Through the leadership of Williams, other CWWG groups around the U.S. gained more legitimate access to previously closed door Pentagon and Army meetings, which was a signal of hope.

Williams won the prestigious 2006 Goldman Environmental Prize of $125,000 for his long and successful efforts in promoting a safer world. It was an award he said he "didn't even know about." In discussing the prize, and the good works of CWWG, his words are sprinkled liberally with "we," and not "I." He remains effectively involved in the work of his organization today, even after suffering a heart attack in December of 2006.

Craig Williams was able to apply lessons he learned from the tragedy in Viet Nam to make today's world a bit safer.

Harley Cannon

'One-Man Band' Musician Sees the Big Picture

Playing music always came easy for Harley Cannon. He was given a little battery piano as a tot, and when he was three he played "Mary had a Little Lamb." With his mother's help, little Harley soon began the process of mastering his family's piano. He still owns that piano today.

Cannon played trumpet in his middle school band and then, in his freshman year at a special residential high school in Maryland, he joined a combo that grandly entertained his peers and others. While there, he benefited from disciplined instruction and support, and he "overcame certain obstacles because they were there, and I had to overcome them."

Cannon, in his early fifties, calls his music ability "a gift from God." He appreciates the blessings he received while a high school student at the Maryland School for the Blind, and what he learned at Prince George's Community College, where he earned an associate's degree in music, studying jazz, piano and trumpet. A resident of Lexington for the last three decades and with his early influences securely entrenched, Harley Cannon joyfully maneuvers his "one-man band" all around Lexington and outlying areas as he seeks to "be a blessing to other people" and, while performing, to feel what he calls "the pleasure of God."

Cannon, one of twins, was born prematurely in 1955, and the over use of oxygen in the incubator caused blindness. His parents desired

photo by Campbell Wood

Harley Cannon

for him to have as normal a life as possible, however. "They gave me every opportunity to be myself and experience what life had to offer. I learned to read and write Braille, which helps me in everyday life," said Cannon. Besides their musical support, young Harley's father also taught him the love of water. "I learned to swim at an early age. I trusted my dad enough that I jumped off a ten-feet diving board when some of my peers were afraid to," he said.

Cannon also recounted a couple of father-son adventures that happened off ocean beaches. "Once, my dad moved my hands away from a lobster just in time as I scuba dived in ten-feet of water. I was in a motor boat by myself another time," he said. "The boat drifted away and I had to start the motor to get it back to shore. It took several tries to head the boat in his direction, but finally I ran the boat right along side him and he grabbed it." Cannon also has water skied as an adult.

Cannon's thirst for challenges, despite his visual impairment, has been a life-long part of his personality. He played in night clubs for several months, and he owned and operated his own recording studio in Lexington for over seventeen years. He has two CD projects out now, one contemporary Christian and the other light jazz. He has "battled addictions and perfectionism all my life," and Cannon said that "his wife deserves a metal for putting up with me for eighteen years." He says he enjoys married life, though, and gives "God the credit for helping me overcome my challenges."

Harley Cannon is a fixture in Lexington. On any day in most any part of town, one might see Cannon—youthful, dark-haired and neatly dressed. He could be stepping on or off a public bus, catching a ride in a friend's car, or simply bopping down the sidewalk, carrying his computer, trumpet, and always with his trusty cane. He may be appearing at a church function or worship service. Cannon might be providing ambience music for a private party, or, at times, the sweet sounds of his uplifting melodies can be heard as he ministers to senior citizens at a nursing home.

On the times he is not performing, Cannon will likely be off by himself, stretching his abundant creativity by composing new songs or poems. Often, he's sharing a laugh with his middle school aged daughter, Amy, or spending quality time with his wife, Ann. Cannon belongs to Toastmasters and enjoys working at the skills of motivational speaking, and he often finds time, he said, "to help out with some organizations that bring awareness to what disabled people have to give to their communities."

Whatever he chooses to do, it's usually worthwhile and designed to lighten the spirits of others. Though carrying an extra burden because of his inability to see, Harley Cannon is always striving, always serving, always growing. In his own darkened world, he persists daily in bringing his own special brand of light. Celebration is his watchword, onward and upward is his mantra. Cannon believes he's on earth for a purpose—to spread a message of optimistic hope.

Jack Pattie, long-time Lexington radio show host for station WVLK, is duly impressed with Cannon and the way he lives. "Beyond his enormous musical talent, his courage is amazing. He does not allow his lack of sight to keep him from doing anything he wants to do. He's an inspiration to all who have had the great fortune to know him."

Though Cannon is capable of playing a wide variety of music, he likes gospel, jazz, and oldies best. He performs with a love for improvising and with lots of dynamics. "I love to add spark to what's going on musically," he said. Cannon listed "Sunny-side Up," "His Eye is on the Sparrow," "Straighten Up and Fly Right," and "I Can See Clearly Now" as some of his favorite performance songs. Of particular fascination to his audiences is his ability to play with one hand on the keyboard—and the other holding, and playing, his trumpet.

In 1996, Cannon performed several times at the Paracultural Olympiad in Atlanta, Georgia. At a recent talent show in London, Kentucky, Cannon picked up a $500 cash prize for his winning performance. He has received sizeable love offerings from recent concerts at local churches. The financial rewards of playing are not routine, however, and not his primary purpose. Ric McGee, director of the Ashland Terrace independent residence for elderly women, in Lexington, shared her knowledge of Cannon's work. "Harley has been coming to our retirement community to entertain for many years—for next to nothing. He generally takes the bus from home, or wherever he is, gets off at Euclid Avenue, and then walks to Ashland Terrace. He is absolutely amazing—fearless, without a whit of self-pity, and so very attuned to the needs of others."

Cannon was recently hired as a worship piano player at Lexington's Northview Baptist Church. He was, as usual, well received and appreciative about it, along with being truly humbled. He couldn't resist a bit of good-natured joking about his good news. "If God can work through a donkey, he can work through me!" he said.

Harley Cannon's One Man Band figures to keep playing. May his good humor and positive attitude open all our eyes a little wider, encourage us to sing a happier song, and look a little more heavenward at our individual blessings.

Bettie L. Johnson

Honored by School that Spurned Her

Bettie L. Johnson at ninety has the look of a woman in her sixties. She also has the sharply dressed, confident look of a modern, successful woman—and she is. Her eyes are intense and radiate intelligence, but they also are approachable and kind eyes.

While sitting comfortably at her desk at the James S. Taylor Nursing Home in downtown Louisville, where she serves as the executive director and tackles issues that plague the elderly in and out of the facility, Johnson pondered thoughtfully questions about her productive life.

"My daddy died when I was four," she spoke softly. "The child next to me was ten years older, so my mother had time to spend with me. She devoted all her time to me, and we read a lot and learned together, you might say."

Growing up in a poor section in Louisville's West End, Bettie Louise Whitenhill carved a niche for herself as an excellent student— an achiever who could hold her own intellectually with anyone. But when it came time to seriously think about going to college, her hometown school was not an option, because the Day Law, enacted in 1904, didn't allow African-American and Caucasian students to sit next to one another in the classroom.

"Black kids were not allowed on the main Belknap campus of the University of Louisville," Johnson said, "so I attended Louisville Municipal College, which was a black college in Louisville that, at that time, was affiliated with the University of Louisville—thereby obeying the Day Law but allowing students to earn credits."

Ironically, what might have seemed to be an inferior education proved otherwise. "We had ninety-eight students, with sixteen teachers. Nine of the teachers had an earned a PhD from prestigious schools," she said. "They came to teach at Municipal because they could not find other college teaching jobs because they were black. We got superior training and there was a low student-teacher ratio."

Bettie L. Johnson

Johnson graduated from LMC in 1936 with a degree in French and English. She then entered Indiana University and graduated with a masters degree in the same subject areas. Soon, Johnson accepted a position at Louisville's Central High School, where she stayed until 1965. At Central, Johnson worked as a teacher, counselor and assistant principal.

An interesting occurrence happened early in Johnson's teaching life. She worked, in a somewhat "hushed" manner, as an administrative assistant in the psychology department at the University of Louisville. It was in the summer of 1952, and she so impressed the department head with her efficiency and hard work that Johnson was asked to join the department—with the caveat that it would be "hidden from the public."

While Johnson was very interested in the offer, she also desired to continue her position at Central High. The school system turned down her request to do both, saying that Johnson would need to resign from her teaching position if she accepted the college offer. Prudently, she stayed at Central because she was her mother's only means of financial support.

Johnson continued her hard work at Central High, and in time took a counselor position in the principal's office. There she performed class scheduling along with a host of other duties. Johnson was successful, but noted a measure of regret for changing positions. "I often think I should have stayed in the classroom to be closer to the kids," Johnson said.

Johnson cared deeply for the poor and those with minority status. She began meeting with community groups while she was still working at Central High School. "The poverty program came out of the idea that neighborhood people would be involved in the decision-making. We spent lots of time in the West End in their homes and basements teaching them about their rights," she said.

Working with a group of Quakers, a successful night school program for dropouts called Learn More, Earn More was organized. The classes prepared students to pass GED exams. Johnson's influence promoted activism. "We helped the neighborhood people march on city hall," she explained, with a hint of pride.

Johnson took a position with the Federal Department of Justice, and in time became a community relations specialist for the purpose of dealing with unrest attributed to school busing in the southeast U.S. region. She had departed Central High with some ruffled feathers in her wake, mainly because of her community activism. "I didn't get a watch or anything," she grinned. "They said that I was subversive. I'll admit it now. I did instigate a lot of things." Johnson later became acting regional director of the program and was based in Atlanta. As a reward for her valuable service she was given extra service credit toward her future retirement. Interestingly, her Atlanta office was on the same floor as Andy Young, noted civil rights activist and former mayor of Atlanta, a person Johnson saw every day.

Bettie Johnson came back to Louisville in the early 1970s and worked for five years as the head of the Child Development Service System, a federal program in thirty-one Louisville schools. In 1977, she became an administrator for a nursing home in Prospect, a suburb of Louisville, in Oldham County. The nursing home had been built by Johnson and James S. Taylor, her husband at the time. Taylor, a successful builder, was motivated to build the facility when he had difficulty admitting his aunt into any similar establishments. "At that time," Johnson said, "I didn't know a thing about running a nursing home."

She did learn, and learned well, but in 1983 another adjustment was in order when her husband died.

Johnson, always determined, decided to continue her work, even though many in a similar situation would have transitioned into retirement mode. "I sold the nursing home and went to work at the nursing home in Louisville that had been built by my husband and his church in 1981." The nursing home was later named after her late husband for his dedication to the healthcare industry.

Today, Johnson serves as the executive director there. Ironically, the building sits directly across the street from Central High Magnet School Academy, where she worked for many years.

She is now married to a man who she refers to as her "blessing." When she was sixty-eight, she married Charlie W. Johnson, who was forty at the time. "He had played football in the NFL and then did well afterwards in the trucking industry," she said. "When he wanted to date me at my age, I thought it was the silliest thing I had ever heard." They were married in 1985.

It has been a good marriage, and with the advantage of their resources the partnership has been able to make many valuable monetary gifts. Ironically, the University of Louisville has been an important recipient, too.

A few years back, Johnson received a lunch invitation from then U of L president John Shumaker. Dr. Shumaker surprised Bettie with the announcement that a state-of-art dormitory was to be built on the university campus and was being named in her honor.

On the day of the grand opening, Bettie Johnson stood in the sunshine on the new dormitory's patio and noted, "It's ironic that I've received such an honor on the campus of a place where at one time I wasn't allowed to attend."

Today, Bettie Johnson is welcome on the University of Louisville campus anytime she pleases. She is often found after hours talking to the students who live in the building that bears her name.

Ruth Blair

Serving Her Hodgenville Amigos

The gently rustic, but proud, landscape of this Kentucky knobs region around Hodgenville is a fitting place to start when one talks about lofty dreams being realized by humble people. One feels in sync with history here, a sense of walking on holy ground. Not holy because Gethsemane monastery is nearby, but because the dirt lies fertile and inviting in the land where a youngster named Abe eked out his iconic foundation—then left, primed and ready, to follow destiny and live a dream.

Occasionally, some come *here* to live out their destiny. Ruth Blair did. Today, she helps others live their dreams.

When young Ruth was a transplant living in Brazil with her single father, she hoped that some day she would be an interpreter faraway at the United Nations in New York. It was a given very early that she wanted to help others. The Portuguese and English languages she already spoke would give her a running start, she reasoned. The picture of what Blair had in mind for her future didn't develop the same as she envisioned, but what did develop might be better. That's because the work she's doing around her community of Hodgenville today, some sixty years later, is international in scope. It involves understanding and mentoring some one hundred Mexican immigrants who seek to integrate themselves into a productive life in small-town Kentucky.

But first, a few words about what Blair did before the Hispanic immigration arrived in recent years. At LaRue County High School in 1965, Ruth started a long and passionate teaching career with husband Garland. While carrying a huge load raising their five children and teaching French and Spanish, she also supported Garland's work with the school's award winning speech teams. The family tacked on thousands of miles on their station wagon in the process of driving students to meets, including a large number in out-of-state locations. Garland died in 1999 and Ruth

Ruth Blair

eventually retired from teaching, but she remained service minded. Consequently, she saw plenty of opportunities to serve when a group of immigrants migrated from Vera Cruz, Mexico to Larue County, Kentucky—experiencing a classic example of culture shock.

Blair's involvement started when the local health department asked her help in administering the Women, Infants and Children program to the immigrants. "They needed someone to help with filling out immunization forms, to help with women's health issues," she said, "and they paid me a small amount to do it." Word spread in the small community, and soon Blair began receiving more requests, especially from the newly arrived Hispanic community. She obliged them, charging no fees and not asking about their citizenship legality situation. "I'm just one of those people who can't say no," Blair said.

She soon found herself with Mexican mothers in the hospital as they gave birth, when they had dental and medical appointments, and when they dealt with car salespersons. When a Hispanic person was involved in a traffic accident—or maybe even sent to jail—Blair was called by authorities to act as translator or to help supply information. She became an advocate for women involved in spousal abuse victimization, helped in child day care facilities, worked with insurance companies, all in the name of helping her Mexican friends.

"Grandma," as Blair became known to the Mexican people, began to appear with immigrants at school conferences, even emailing teachers regarding her "clients" and their needs.

Today, Ruth Blair's work continues full bore. She counts at least 100 in her network, with over half of them children. A quick look at her well-used planner shows the depth of her involvement. "I know all the names of the people I work with and I have their addresses and phone numbers written down in this book," she said.

In 2006, she added eleven new names to her list from the new-born she saw come into this world. Blair confers on her clients the same sense of humanity that she would give to any of her friends around LaRue County. "These are people who want the same things we all want—a better life and a better life for their kids, " she explained.

Blair's act of love is full-time. She spends at least forty to fifty hours per week, with little or no pay. In addition, she is active with the Spanish mass in her Catholic church in Hodgenville, Our Lady of Mercy, and even finds time to play cards with friends, though she may be frequently interrupted by phone calls. The mileage she puts on her car per week averages about 250 and she has a super-sized cell phone minute plan. She handles each call with patience and tenderness.

Recently, an unexpected act of kindness was bestowed on Blair. "I received a call from a local car dealer, and some people, who the dealer would not identify specifically, had given me a new car, a 2006 Ford Fuson," she said. "At first, I thought it was a joke." The car, now driven on the roads around Hodgenville and even sometimes to Elizabethtown carrying immigrant passengers she serves, came with a note indicating appreciation from her former school students who were involved with Garland and her speech teams.

Blair doesn't really understand what all the fuss is about, however. "I don't see anything special about what I do," she said, "because anybody else would do the same thing." She might get some disagreement there. Giving up one's retirement years in complete service to others unrelated to her family is not only unusual, but few would blame those who take a pass on those kind of acts.

Asked where her passion originated, Blair is quite sure she knows. "It came from my father, who was a chemist down in Brazil. My mother died when I was young, but my father was always involved in civic things like the Boy Scouts, Red Cross and the Rotary," she said. "He was a Catholic, a non-practicing one who didn't go to church, but he always helped others."

Does Blair see a time soon when she will slow down from the pace she keeps—when she'll decide to *really* retire? "Not really, unless I lose my health," she said. Then she paused. "No, I'll step down when the next generation is able to take over and do for their own families."

With the support and great modeling that Ruth Blair presents, the next generation of Mexican people around Hodgenville should be quite capable. Besides, we already know that the ground around these parts grows greatness.

Calvin Ray Johnson

Singer Overcomes Adversity to Wow Audiences

It's a clear Saturday evening night at a night spot on the Blue Moon Highway, near Leitchfield. The band has warmed, the lights are glaring and the crowd is buzzing in anticipation. In moments, the star of the show appears, as promised. He comes rockin', shakin' and beltin' out a country favorite.

Soon, he's worked the crowd to a near frenzy—and he's doing it from the confines of a wheelchair, no less.

Few in tonight's audience focus on the wheelchair, though. Few notice it as an obstacle. They came to be entertained, and they are. Simply put, all are having a good time down at Calvin Ray's Live Music, and they'll be back again..

Calvin Ray Johnson not only won every karaoke contest imaginable a few years back, he would have been hard to beat in a smiling contest, too. "Guess I'm pretty energetic and upbeat," he said with a smile, "and I guess I've always been into performing." As he smiled, revealing a beautiful set of shiny white teeth, he spoke appreciatively, "I'm grateful to God for giving me the gift to sing. I'm grateful, too, for the support of my parents to help me realize my dreams."

Realized dreams for the twenty-seven-year-old, who battles Duchenne muscular dystrophy, are many. First, he has outlived the expected lifespan, which, on average, is about twenty-one. He has cut compact discs, including the recent *Take That Chance,* which features his popular single, "Should've Been Singing Rock of Ages." Calvin

Ray performed on-stage in Hollywood at the 2001 and 2003 Jerry Lewis Telethon, where he performed a duet with Kermit the Frog. He again performed in the national event in September, 2007, electrifying the studio crowd with his rendition of the Frank Sinatra's classic, "My Way."

Calvin Ray has won four talent contests at The Nashville Palace and recently appeared in Nashville at the Midnight Jamboree. He is a two-time Muscular Dystrophy Association achievement award

Calvin Ray Johnson

winner and was named Kentucky's goodwill ambassador. Perhaps his most noteworthy accomplishment is that he has a permanent place to perform musically every Saturday night with his own house musical group, The Blue Moon Highway Band.

Calvin Ray's Live Music, which seats 800, opened in 2004. Built by his construction savvy father, Max, with the support of his mother, Debbie, it has a restaurant serving full course meals before Saturday's show time. "It will rival what you find in Branson," said Earl Owens, Calvin's publicist. "It is a state-of-the art entertainment center that hosts such as Don Williams, Pam Tillis, and Little Jimmy Dickens." Besides performing with his band, Calvin Ray invites fledgling newcomers to perform. The Leitchfield area, where Max Johnson grew up, was chosen over the Mt. Washington area, outside Louisville, where the Johnson's live. "There were already plenty of jamboree places around Mt. Washington, so we decided to build down there," Calvin Ray said.

Life began in a pretty normal fashion for young Calvin Ray. He played little league basketball and baseball, but, at eight-years-old, he started falling down frequently. Soon, he received the Duchenne diagnosis, with the dreaded symptoms of generalized muscular weakness and wasting of tissue. Four years later he was wheelchair bound. "The hardest thing was giving up sports," he said. "I liked to do art and draw, so I did that kind of thing through high school."

When he reached eighteen, his new art seemed to drop in his lap. "I had always enjoyed Elvis and '50s music. I bought tapes and sang along with them at my house. My audience was pretty much just Mom and Dad," he said with a grin. "And so one night I entered a karaoke contest, did some Elvis, and won. Lots of my friends came to me and told me they were surprised I could sing like that."

That experience was the start, and the encouragement, he needed to pursue a music career. There were more karaoke gigs, local jamborees and MDA events. Since 1998, Calvin Ray Johnson has become a well-respected singer who performs country, '50s and even some gospel music. His career is on an upward path, and he has more dreams—even with his health concerns. "I'd like to get some radio air time for some of my CD's, and I'd really like to be on the Grand Old Opry some day," he said.

Jim Vest, Calvin Ray's music producer, told The Hendersonville (Tennessee) Star News that Johnson "is a young singer that has a lot of energy and is willing to work hard for what he wants." So far, with support from many people, a talented ability to sing and an inspiring, positive attitude, Calvin Ray Johnson is right on schedule for achieving what he, and his growing audience desires.

Betty Rushford

Fighting an Intrusion on Life

Kentucky native Betty Rushford was taught long ago that her Christian faith didn't guarantee a life of ease and good fortune.

If she hadn't received proof already, she found out for sure when what she calls "an intrusion on life" occurred in her family. The devastation inflicted might surely have destroyed many ordinary people, but a simple, yet strong, faith in God helped make Rushford's experience become a blessing for thousands—both in the U.S. and in other countries.

It started in 1986 when her youngest son, Dino, was diagnosed with HIV, the deadly AIDS virus, after living a gay lifestyle. Driven by fear and phobias, accounts of negative reactions to the condition were common all across the nation. Many were fearful of the contagious nature of the virus through exchanging of bodily fluids, infected needles, and sex. Many people had inaccurate information about spreading the virus, and some manifested pure hatred toward homosexuals.

Sadly, and for whatever reasons, it happened in a small Kentucky town where Rushford's family lived. Quoting from her book, *Mercy Triumphs,* Rushford said, "We didn't know what to expect but we never dreamed that the people I grew up with, went to church with, lived next door to, and worked with would react the way they did... Our family doctor told me that some family members had called him with concern about having eaten some food I had cooked for the family Christmas dinner... People began to call us on the phone and tell us to 'get out of town and quit spreading AIDS.' Some would drive by the house, throw things in the yard and yell out abusive phrases. They would also drive by my business and yell out these abuses."

Feeling they had no realistic choice, the Rushford family moved southward to the much larger city of Chattanooga, Tennessee. There Rushford, through prayer and support from loved ones, pondered the experience through the eyes of her devout Christian faith. Questions arose as she and family dealt with

Betty Rushford

the pain of rejection and Dino's grave illness, plus financial stresses caused by the abrupt, unforeseen changing of residence. Why did this happen? What could be learned as a result? How could these circumstances be used for a greater, positive purpose?

Answers began to slowly emerge as she hit on the idea of an AIDS victim support organization. In 1989, with help from her place of worship, Bethel Temple Assembly of God, Rushford developed a ministry called Channels of Love. It's aims were to provide counseling and support-group meetings, hot meals, financial assistance, plus other elements like community awareness. Again, there were difficult challenges as the ministry took root. "We could not get a public place for various reasons. Some weren't available four nights a month. Some didn't want people with AIDS sitting in their chairs. So we had to meet in our homes," Rushford said. That worked well for a while, but more and more clients came, too many to continue the program in individual homes.

Channels of Love soon found a suitable building for $50,000. Suitable, but it was not affordable. Betty Rushford perceived what happened next as providential. A local businessman with a heart for AIDS victims donated $25,000 and the organization worked hard to raise most of the rest. The process was helped along the way by the support of 1993's Miss America, Leanza Cornett, who appeared at a Channels fund-raising banquet.

Rushford opened her arms wide for people dying with AIDS in the Chattanooga community. She took to heart the characteristics of true, unconditional love written in 1 Corinthians 13: 4-8. She dealt with the unpleasantness of persons with poor hygiene, their depression and thoughts of suicide, and their often lack of financial resources. She became the only friend some of the patients had. Betty Rushford's model of servanthood to other volunteers in Channels of Love invigorated them.

Meanwhile, as she was serving AIDS victims outside her family, son Dino had gotten progressively worse. In 1997, Rushford resigned from the organization she started to take care of her dying son. "I had always told myself that when his turn came that I would quit and be by his side," she said. The devotion to her son entailed changing his colostomy bag, as well as being an unrelenting and faithful encourager to him. During those final days with Dino, Betty saw him undergo a special moment of epiphany as he came to terms with his own religious faith. She remembers fondly. "From that day on he was changed, truly changed. He let go of all the hurts, unforgiveness, and other hindrances. I got back that little boy that I had given birth to, for the head injury he suffered in the accident he suffered at age twelve had changed his personality so drastically that he was a different person." Dino died in 1998 and was buried on June 8, his mother's birthday.

After some time for healing, Betty Rushford followed what she considered God's will, and in the year 2000 organized Betty Rushford Ministries, Inc. Two years later, Project: A Haven of Hope, was established and operated under that parent organization. Today, her ministry of reaching out to those suffering from HIV/AIDS is thriving and touches other continents around the world. All those serving with her do so as volunteers. Some 700 pastors and church leaders have been trained in AIDS seminars, and more than 8000 sick people have been treated in such places as Kenya, Ghana, Nigeria, Tanzania, Northern India and Haiti. In Siaya, Kenya, Betty Rushford Ministries has opened a medical clinic that is designed to serve 25,000 with proper care, unlike what had been offered in that area before. The organization also presents a mentoring seminar called Mentoring His Handmaidens, designed "to assist women who feel the call of God upon their lives and desire some guidance."

Rushford has seen a whole host of people's lives gain hope and spiritual fulfillment through the suffering of her family after "an intrusion on life" visited them. Even now, she continues to see herself as God's instrument and unworthy of praise. "I don't see myself as a hero but just doing what I feel I must do. If it wasn't for Jesus, I wouldn't have accomplished anything. He's the hero," she said.

Jim Palm

Given the 'Opportunity' to Save a Life

The way Jim Palm explains it, thousands of people die everyday who have not had the opportunity to save another person's life.

"I was given the opportunity," said Palm. He has a twelve-inch scar on his abdomen to prove it, the remnants of surgery performed in 1999 in order to transplant one of his kidneys to his younger sister, Melody Hofmann, who needed a new organ or she would die. She is now living an active and full life. So is Palm.

A band director, principal, and school superintendent in Kentucky for the last three decades, Palm has always handled life's challenges with strong religious faith, which, he said, "is something my family has always had. I believe everyone is put on this earth for a purpose, and it's our job to find what it is."

Palm's disarming sense of humor, along with his now deceased father's positive influence and the support of his wife, Beth, have also been personal mainstays of his full and gracious life.

The process that led to Palm's act of sacrifice started in 1986 when Melody was diagnosed with chronic renal failure. Doctors said she would likely need to undergo a kidney transplant in two to three years, *if* a suitable donor was found. When Palm was asked if he'd be willing to help Melody with the gift of a kidney when the time came, his answer was unhesitatingly clear: "You're my sister. I'm going to take care of you. The answer is yes and will always be yes."

He requested one condition, however. He didn't want to talk about it until it was necessary— meaning at the time it was needed. "I process things better that way," Palm said. Following strict diet guidelines from her doctors, Melody continued without the need to have a transplant for over twelve years—an amazing tribute to her personal discipline.

When Palm's sister's time of urgency arrived in 1999, the recent past had already made things difficult for Palm. His father, Ray Palm, who son Jim called "my best

Jim Palm

friend," died in 1997. The son is an inheritor of his father's humorous wit, and it was on display as Jim talked about the events leading up to surgery. "The doctor explained the full details of what I'd have to expect," he said, "and asked if I had any questions." Palm's deadpan answer was "Will it hurt my male modeling career?"

The doctor also conveyed to Palm shortly before the surgery that he would be free to walk out the door before the surgery, and, understandably, "No one would say a word about it." Palm laughed when he remarked that the hospital officials "then put bars on the door before I could leave." While Palm's father was not there physically when his son went through the challenges involved, he was nonetheless important. "My father was there spiritually," Palm said.

As discomforting as such an operation is, there were even more complications than could be reasonably expected. In an age where malpractice suits are not uncommon, where many people feel an exaggerated sense of entitlement, Jim Palm goes against the grain. As he was being readied for surgery, the 280-pounder's legs were lifted, then fell when the manual turn handle malfunctioned. "They called a mechanic in to help, but he couldn't fix it," said Palm, this time not joking. It was decided to transfer Palm to another bed, and in the process he was dropped, causing a tube to jerk out of his throat, which resulted in extreme pain. "When I talked, I sounded like Daffy Duck for a while," Palm joked. Then, during the complex surgery, what is called a "nicked nerve" was experienced. Today, the surgical wound still leaves Palm with moments of discomfort. "It has lessened as the years have passed," he said.

To Palm's credit, there is no trace of bitterness. It's just not his way. "How could I be angry with a group of people who were trying to save my sister's life," he said matter-of-factly.

As doctors predicted, the kidney transplant brought relief for the recipient—and made the donor sick, at least for a while. Palm missed six weeks of being at his Warsaw office as Gallatin County's school superintendent, though he did some paperwork in his home. Over time, Palm slimmed down as he ate healthier and added more exercise to his daily schedule. After retiring several years ago and keeping busy selling real estate, he decided to come back to the education profession, where he now is the superintendent of the Southgate Independent School District, near Newport.

Palm lives with his wife and mother in Claryville, near Alexandria, at the same house where he was raised. The family is active in the Lutheran Church.

Palm doesn't see himself as a hero, though you won't convince his sister Melody Hofmann that he isn't. "I send him cards sometimes," she said, "but he doesn't want me to brag on him to others. What he did for me gave me new life. It also helped encourage me with my own husband, who had an undiagnosed medical problem. Jim is my hero whether he wants to hear it or not."

For Jim Palm, a little humor to soften daily trials, some support from his family and the encouraging spirit of his father—plus, a happy, vibrant sister is enough for him.

Darlene Snyder

In Sickness and in Health

Darlene fell in love with Mike Snyder when she was seven. Her adoration for him was not returned for a long time, however. Mike didn't notice her until she was sixteen, and then they started dating. Even then, there were complications. "At first, he started standing me up," she said, grinning, "but finally, I guess he came to his senses."

Today, it would be a real stretch to find a stronger marriage and a tighter bond than between this couple. Darlene saw the light early. She has demonstrated her love to Mike over and over. He has received, appreciated, and loved her back. "That woman has saved my life," he remarked. Truly, as Mike knows, it's hard to turn away the kind of love that has saved your life.

Nowadays, you might see the two lovebirds riding their motorcycle together on the curvy, rural roadways of Kentucky, usually not far from their home in Kirksville, in Madison County. They have fun, enjoy pleasant scenery and grow in their companionship. They stop a lot, too, not because they want to stop, but because they must—for Mike, who has some health issues. Thankfully, they're always well-prepared for the stops. Darlene sees to that. She's loved him since she was seven.

Since 1994, Mike hasn't been well. For years he dealt with pancreatitis, colitis and also had gall bladder surgery. "He was in the hospital a while, got taken care of, then was out. But then he'd have to go back," Darlene said. It was aggravating for Mike, but he continued to work hard driving heavy equipment for the Madison County Road

Department. "That's all I'd ever known," he said. He also had musical talent that he generously shared with others. He played in local churches, including his own, Kirksville Baptist. He regularly appeared at several nursing homes. He played the guitar, banjo, dulcimer, and mandolin and sang with undying enthusiasm of his religious faith. Unfortunately, his health difficulties began to worsen. A condition in the colon called ulcerative colitis caused ulcers to develop, and Mike became, said Darlene, "one sick puppy."

Mike & Darlene Snyder

The toughest of times began in 2003 when Mike's mother died. He also became sicker. Remembering the many relatively happy years of marriage, church, a good job, family and raising an only child, circumstances were now changing drastically. And even though the couple held tightly to their strong, religious faith, "Everything was falling apart," Darlene said. In 2004, Mike's father died. That same year doctors performed a protocollectomy procedure, an operation that removed the entire colon and rectum. A "J-pouch," or reservoir for collection of bodily wastes, was formed by stretching the small intestine. The procedure is bold and is not without complications. The pouch is small, and predictably, necessitated frequent emptying, meaning an inordinate number of trips to the bathroom—sometimes as many as twenty to thirty times per day.

Without fail, Darlene was a constant, encouraging companion. Through surgeries and regular hospital visits, home convalescing and all times between, her declared love at age seven demonstrated itself over and over. That included helping Mike clean himself when accidents occurred outside the bathroom. Often during his hospital stays, Darlene, at his side, helped Mike with much of his cleaning. That included the wastes that were on the floor, on the sheets, and his gown. "The nurses tended to do less of it since I helped, and it got to be a process for me. I would gather his clothes, go to a nearby laundry mat, (and) then bring them back to his room clean. That also gave me a bit of a break," she said.

On one particular occasion, "one of the worst days since we married," Darlene said, Mike became consumed with both pain and frustration. He begged to be taken home from the hospital, where he "would end it all with his gun." Darlene, in anguish herself, did all she could to soothe and encourage him as a nurse sedated him. "After he received the Valium and was asleep, I sat beside his bed in an uncomfortable chair and cried uncontrollably for hours," she said The chilling episode passed, then Darlene made her way downstairs to the chapel—and welcome relief came. "I allowed God's peace to wash over me," she said.

After his long stays in the hospital were less frequent, and when they were in the privacy of their home, Darlene thought about ways to help Mike be more comfortable. One idea began to make sense in regard to Mike's solitary bathroom time. The time, she reasoned, might be used for greater gain.

Darlene would simply join him there.

"I pulled a chair into the bathroom so I could talk with Mike," she said very matter-of-factly. Though not under the most pleasant environment, the two discussed, and shared, typical items that long married people converse about: their wants, their needs, their son who graduated from Bible college, church life, the price of gasoline, local news—and, their caring sentiment toward each other. "When my friends found out I was doing this, they thought it was funny, but sweet," Darlene said.

It shouldn't surprise that a love that began at age seven often has a history of funny and sweet things accumulated. Another poignant, even humorous story when the couple visited a favorite local restaurant. "Mike did a fine job of not overeating. He excused himself and went to the bathroom, and he had been gone for some time when I checked on him. He was in one of the messes that would be too graphic to describe," she said. "In order to keep other people from seeing the result of his mess, I told him I would walk real close behind him and we could head straight for the car. We shuffled along and did not look to see if others were watching." Was it a traumatic situation for the two? "We have laughed about it on many occasions and wondered what the people thought when they saw us walking like that," she said.

Though doctors hoped that the J-pouch procedure would allow Mike to return to work, cold practicality made it almost impossible— there would be way too many interruptions to be effective. Today, Mike spends most of his time at home, where he does some of the couple's cooking, helps with household chores, writes songs and plays his music.

Darlene, from her workplace in the district court office in Richmond, checks on him often and is always ready to rush home in an urgent time. She loves to take church leadership roles, but for Mike, has had to curtail many of them. When Mike feels well enough, the couple gets in gear with their Yamaha 1300 motorcycle for a trip in the country. She prepares a bag of supplies and knows full well that their trip may be a short one, but even a small time together, having fun, is important to them. It's been that way for Darlene since she was seven.

Darlene is a multi-tasker extraordinaire. Despite her full-time job at the Madison County District Court and total dedication to one Mike Snyder and her church work, she is a fledgling published writer. She had a magazine article published in *Kentucky Monthly* about their motorcycle adventures. She is currently working on a book dealing with how to be a pastor's wife, with inspiration coming from her daughter-in-law, married to her pastor son.

In describing Darlene and her uncommon devotion to his needs, Mike Snyder speaks eloquently: "Darlene is an ordinary person who has been placed in an extraordinary predicament and has faced the challenge with grace and dignity."

She truly has, since way back when she was seven.

Harold Slade

Bringing Order to the Past

The clip-clop sound of one's shoes on hard wood is muted, some-what, by articles on walls and on tables. There is the cloth of military uniforms and other old-time apparel; near life-size wooden silhouettes of a lady and son doing outside chores; yellowing signs, new signs; and opened books with a script that shames the modern. One can see the pictures of graduating Cynthiana High School classes taken before most of us were born, and there are soft-featured, rosy-faced dolls in a Raggedy Ann exhibit that signals young and simple fun. All the items titillate the nostalgic senses of visitors to the Cynthiana-Harrison County Museum.

There is another strong sensation, too. Everywhere you walk, there's the feeling of order—meticulous order. Everything in the museum, it seems, is in place and planned, and it has an almost sym-metrical quality. You can tell that Harold Slade has his designer's hand in this impressive project.

Slade, born in 1919 in Bourbon County, started his chronicling of history hobby when he got interested in his family tree in the mid 1970s. He visited libraries and court houses all around the area as well as recording information from members of his family. He has at least thirty-five binders containing his Slade and wife Dorothy's Florence genealogy, with each work containing prolific detail and neat, block-manuscript writing. Not content with the endless hours spent on his immediate family's lineage, he's been known to help tell the story of others not related to him. One such was an elderly gentleman. "Ol' Mr. McCauley could talk all day telling stories," said Slade, "but he wasn't ever going to write anything down. So I told him if he'd give me the story, I'd write it down for him." He later handed to Mr. McCauley, now deceased, a product that showed his typical quality of workmanship.

In recent years, the local Cynthiana-Harrison County Trust, Inc. commissioned Slade to put together a similar chronicle of Harrison County military veterans. "We collected about

Harold Slade

seventy stories of our veterans from this area. Some of them I wrote myself, and some were already written." Slade dismissed the idea of producing a hard back collection, saying "we're always getting more stories to add." He found time in the early 1990s to lead in the restoration of the Abdel Cemetary, a graveyard in rural Harrison County where his great, great, great grandparents lie. "The place was really a jungle," he remarked, "and I had to clean up and put back together old gravestones. It looks pretty good now, and people can come and walk through it."

The story of how the Cynthiana-Harrison County Museum materialized also started back in the early '90s. "The Trust was having a lot of meetings," Slade said, "and we were doing a lot of talking. Somebody said, 'Let's do something.' So we decided to work on getting a history museum going here."

With his cousin, George Slade, sharing a common passion, the two began searching for two things: items from bygone days to exhibit and a place to exhibit them. Martha Barnes, another important Trust member, helped them find a place. "Robert Poindexter rented us a north side room of his vacant building on Walnut Street for $100 per month," explained Harold, "and, we received permission to have any items we wanted from the old J&R Drugs Store on Pike Street, which had gone out of business."

The gathering of items from the drug store had its light moments. "Some of the stuff was just junk waiting to be carried off to the dumpster, but some of it was good, too. George and I crawled around in their basement and attic. It was real dirty. We came out looking like a couple of miners," Harold said with a laugh. "We found an old life-sized Santa Claus they once had on display. There were parts scattered all over the place, and we almost threw it away. But I gathered the pieces and tinkered with them at home and got it to start moving side to side again." The two transported many of the items with a two-wheel push-cart and had the unenviable task of cleaning the grime and soot from them. They salvaged Timex watch cases that proved very valuable for displaying. At the same time, word spread about the project and more donations became available. A stained-glass window was garnered from the old train depot and some useful items came from an old school building in the area.

When the museum officially opened on July 22, 1994, there still were not many historical items to see, though they were neatly displayed. "We had about fifteen or twenty pieces to show and we had nerve enough to call it a museum," Harold recalled with a grin.

Today, however, the community museum is thriving in a larger building down the street, with thousands of Harrison County remembrances of the past proudly on exhibit. The city and county governments provide some of the funding. A steady flow of visitors come, most in awe of the local project. Its success has surely been a product of a lot of people's contributions, but the work of Harold Slade, even after the death a few year's back of his colleague, George, has been especially exemplary and time-tested.

Because of his vision and hard work, he can add color to individual tours of the museum. Though it's a bit of a fancy term for Slade, he is the "curator," the one who patrons most ask their questions about the items in the museum. Visitors come through the doors every Friday and Saturday.

Because the Cynthiana-Harrison County Museum is firmly up and running, Harold Slade has more time to give to Gristmill Day in May, another project he helped start along with a local man. On Gristmill Day, the community of Cynthiana celebrates the tradition of grinding corn meal the old-fashioned way.

Slade also has more time to keep the Abdel Cemetary neat and orderly, which just seems the natural thing for him to do.

John Rosenberg

Balancing the Scales of Justice in Eastern Kentucky

John Rosenberg has been in the middle of significant historical times since he was born to Jewish parents into the political turmoil of 1931 Germany.

Many years later, in another part of the world, America, he helped *make* history. He participated, as a lawyer, in the great civil rights battles of the 1960s in the Deep South. In the last three decades Rosenberg, living and working in the quaint, Appalachian town of Prestonsburg, Kentucky—has spread his sphere of influence even further. He's touched lives in the Appalachian Mountains of eastern Kentucky and beyond in a way that will be forever significant.

The three different times and places have a strong connection to each other. The first and second helped form him, the latter helped define him.

"I was born in Magdeburg, Germany during the days when Adolf Hitler was rising to power," said Rosenberg. The family lived in a Jewish community, next to a synagogue. The father was a school teacher and a lay leader at the religious building. What happened as a child in the middle of the night, November 11, 1938, is indelibly imprinted in John Rosenberg's psyche. It has been called "Night of the Broken Glass," or *Kristallnacht*.

"We watched as storm troopers proceeded to build a bonfire of all the holy books in the synagogue, and then they dynamited the building.

The next morning the Nazis arrested my father and took him to the concentration camp in Buchenwald," he said.

After a week, Rosenberg's father was released and returned to the family, and they were able to move to an internment camp in Holland for a year. After that year, his family was able to arrange passage on a boat to the United States, one that Rosenberg called "the last boat bound for the United States, before Germany invaded Holland in the early stages of the Second World War." Still reeling

John Rosenberg

from the rude uprooting, but joyful about arriving—safe, but with few resources—in the city of New York, the Rosenbergs awaited a new life.

Soon, the Rosenbergs migrated to their adopted country's southern region, to Spartanburg, South Carolina. There, the father gained work sweeping floors at a shirt factory, then quickly began a promotion process. That same work ethic, plus an astute intelligence, enabled son John to acquire scholarships, then to graduate with a bachelor's degree from Duke University. A four year stint in the U.S. Air Force followed, then Rosenberg worked in sales for a Philadelphia chemical manufacturer. But more noble instincts took over, and John Rosenberg headed southward again, this time to the University of North Carolina Law School. He graduated in 1962, and a most productive public service career was ready to begin.

Predictably, Rosenberg was drawn toward issues of justice, particularly for those with little power because of their status in life, ie, the poor, racial minorities, and those who, by birth and culture, unwittingly invited prejudice against themselves. He became a part of the Civil Rights Division of the U.S. Department of Justice during a time when the U.S. experienced tremendous social upheaval. It was the time of Martin Luther King, voting literacy tests, and racial violence. Rosenberg, working under mentor John Doar, was part of the team that prosecuted the murderers of three civil rights workers in the noted *U.S. v. Price* case in 1967. An acclaimed movie about the case, called *Mississippi Burning*, was later produced in 1988. From 1962 to 1970, Rosenberg handled major cases involving voting rights, school desegregation, public accommodations, and employment discrimination cases largely in the South. In a time when core values were challenged, and needed to be—often against bitterly hostile resistance—John Rosenberg was positioned squarely in the dynamics of fundamental civil rights change in America.

In 1970, after leaving the Justice Department, Rosenberg received a request to come work with a group of lawyers to address what were called "some serious legal issues in central Appalachia." Rosenberg, his wife Jean and small child were camping in Canada at the time, but soon headed south in their '66 Peugeot—on their way to little Prestonsburg, Kentucky. The family stayed in a camping site outside the town, made connections to the principals involved in the federal legal services program that would be expanded into eastern Kentucky, then, as Rosenberg likes to say, "We never left."

Rosenberg was hired as the deputy director of the Appalachian Research and Defense Fund (Appalred), headquartered in Charleston, West Virginia, for the Kentucky operations office in Prestonsburg. Appalred was formed as a federally financed legal services program, helping those without the resources to hire their own lawyers for civil matters. The Kentucky office, with Rosenberg at the helm, would cover a thirty-seven-county area in eastern Kentucky, and by 1973, Rosenberg's agency would be funded independently of the Charleston office.

At Appalred, Rosenberg began to assemble a competent, committed staff of lawyers that reached forty-eight by 1981. A large cadre of interns and volunteers from a wide variety of law schools were brought on board by virtue of Rosenberg's sterling reputation. Around the region, ten Appalred offices operated, and they were effective, serving sometimes as many as 7000 clients per year. Tackled by Rosenberg and his passionate cavalry for the poor were family law, consumer matters, housing, health law and disability issues involving Medicaid and SSI matters, environmental law and coal mine health and safety.

A highly significant victory occurred in 1988 in what John Rosenberg termed "the death knell of the interpretation of the broad form deed." That deed, according to the Kentucky courts, allowed harmful surface mining to take place without the landowner's consent. Appalred's lawyers had tried to overturn this judicial interpretation for year's without success. The death knell was a constitutional amendment that effectively required landowner consent before surface mining could take place. The amendment's language was written by Rosenberg and his staff. It passed largely through the efforts of a grassroots citizens group, Kentuckians for the Commonwealth, with ninety-two percent of Kentucky voters agreeing. Another important case involved an action in the 1970s against building a dam on the Red River, which would have displaced many poor people and destroyed a pristine part of the Red River Gorge. In several other cases, Appalred's Mine Safety Project won victories for miners when they complained about safety conditions. Appalred's work to make sure public school students received free text books resulted in a legislative victory for low-income people. There are many more stories, but Rosenberg and Appalred's greatest legacy is perhaps in the thousands of individual stories of appreciative, now hopeful, clients in the region.

Rosenberg's influence in the Prestonsburg community has also been, in a word, exemplary.

The community of David was dying. A former coal camp about ten miles from Prestonsburg, it's condition again stirred Rosenberg's social justice sensibilities. Said Rosenberg, "The houses were owned by a group of local businessmen who collected rent but refused to do any substantial repair work. After a series of community meetings, we incorporated the David Community Development Corporation (DCDC), which bought 'the town'—about forty houses and the surface area surrounding the town from ridge to ridge. Over the next few years, the DCDC financed and sold the houses to the resident-renters, built about twenty new low income and moderate income homes, developed a new water and sewer system, and supported the development of a model alternative school for high school dropouts called the David School." Rosenberg was part of virtually all of the legal work required for the development.

One wonders where Rosenberg finds time to accomplish so many things, but his help in promoting improved science education in the area—both for children and parents—resulted in the East Kentucky Science Center on the Prestonsburg campus of Big Sandy Community and Technical College. It's ironic that Rosenberg's bachelor's degree from Duke was in chemistry, and not political science, but knowledge in both fields led him, as chairman of the center's governing board, to propose a building including a planetarium, an exhibit hall and a science classroom, and it was accomplished in 1997. To date, over 40,000 students have taken advantage of the science center and it's services. "Our original idea was to acquire science materials and disperse them to schools, but it became a bigger project," Rosenberg said. "We hope to see young people be inspired to get into the field of science through this experience."

Rosenberg also was influential in establishing a local project that improved housing conditions in eastern Kentucky. "We established a successful low income housing project to focus on home repairs for our citizens," he said. The program is essentially driven by volunteers and has made a difference in the daily lives of hundreds. Rosenberg's wife, Jean, has also been a tireless supporter of his initiatives for the needs of others less fortunate. She has directed a program for single parent homemakers, many who have been abused, to help provide educational opportunity and financial assistance, plus emotional support.

For John Rosenberg, it has been a productive life. A man blessed by new opportunities in America after being pushed from his homeland, he has returned the blessing a thousandfold. Forgoing much higher income and the prestige of a more high profile law practice,

Rosenberg chose to use his bright mind to help form brighter futures and offer hope to multitudes of common and decent folk who needed only a little boost along the way. "Lawyering uphill," a term he often uses to describe Appalred's difficult cases over the years, might also apply in general to the good work he has done in Appalachia, where he has made a positive difference for future generations in eastern Kentucky.

Shad Baker

Blazing the Pine Mountain Trail

In 1996, Jenkins-resident Shad Baker and his backpacking friends waited out a rainstorm under a roof-leaking shelter in the Great Smokey Mountains. They were in the midst of a seven-day excursion, and nearly every day had been wet and foggy, with very little promised "beautiful scenery" visible.

Frustrated, someone in the group said, "You know, we've driven all these hours down here to see nothing. We live in the mountains back home. Why don't we do this back home?" The group brainstormed a little while. They agreed that the familiar Pine Mountain range, where they lived, would be well suited to a long-distance trail. The aggravation of the rain break turned into a good-luck charm. Starting with that conversation, Kentucky is now well on its way to possessing a 120-mile hiking route along the Pine Mountains that stretches from Breaks Interstate Park, outside Elkhorn City, to Cumberland Gap, near Middlesboro.

The first official meeting of the hiking activists, now known as the Pine Mountain Trail Conference, was held in Ross Kegan's coal company office in 1997. An action plan developed quite quickly because of two main factors. First, Shad Baker was Letcher County's Cooperative Extension Agent for Agriculture and Natural Resourses, and "community development" was a viable part of his job description. Kegan had some connections in place with his experiences working with agencies on mountain issues. The National Park Service, U.S. Forest Service and interested individuals from Virginia soon joined in investigating the possibilities. At first, the group received a series of relatively small, but helpful grants to start the project. One significant development happened with the aid of former governor Paul Patton. The Pine Mountain Trail gained official recognition by receiving a government sponsored Millennium Legacy grant. That act designated the trail as one which represents the past, present and future of the state, making the project eligible for a greater range of grants.

Shad Baker

Still, Baker and Kegan began doing manual labor out on the trail "with only three volunteers, and some people didn't think the whole idea would ever amount to anything," Baker recalled. "Thinking piecemeal," the term Baker used to describe his mindset when the project started, soon changed to something more grandiose when a county-extension related trip to Washington, D.C. resulted in some unexpected, but positive news. "We were sitting in Congressman Hal Roger's office and an aide asked us if there's anything they could do for us back home," Baker remembered. Several months later, with the words of the aide nearly forgotten, Baker was sitting in his Whitesburg office and received a phone call of congratulations. "The caller had read in the local paper that our project had been awarded a one million dollar grant through Hal Roger's work. We had no idea that it was going to happen. It was almost like 'divine appointment,' and now, we could start thinking big," Baker said.

Baker quickly went about the business of working with the government to gain private property easements for the trail or to buy property outright, an arduous but absolutely necessary task. He received much support from his area extension director, David Adams. Baker also embarked upon a busy schedule of speaking to individuals and groups regarding the project, where "good people were fearful about losing their land and would get upset." In those cases, Baker used his easy-going, sincere nature, plus his regional roots to cultivate relationships and quell misunderstandings. It worked, and momentum for the endeavor increased.

Aided by enthusiastic involvement from the American Hiking Society, the volunteer force began to grow quickly. The organization committed to send groups of fifteen each week for five weeks a year over a five-year period, allowing Baker's plans to solidify for the foreseeable future. Some of the individuals involved desired to come back on their own to do more work. Boy Scout groups and similar groups became part of the force. As publicity for the trail project grew, more and more individuals stepped forward, including people with passionate political views—both conservative and liberal. "We have had volunteers who worked together even though they wore their politics on their sleeves," Baker said with a grin. Hot discussions along the trail are still common, yet real progress continued in making the Pine Mountain Trail passable for all hikers. Kegan explained a reason for the unusual marriage of the two groups that has seemed to work well. "People have different reasons for wanting to be helping on the trail," he said. "Some are strong environmentalists and others love being outdoors and active."

From humble beginnings, the Pine Mountain Trail project is now functioning like a well-oiled machine. Recently, it has received groups of volunteers from the University of Wisconsin. To date, Baker noted that "over a thousand volunteers have taken part in the project, and it is hard work." At this time, at least forty-five miles of the 120 are marked and ready for humans to navigate by foot—and experience Kentucky's natural mountain beauty. It is hoped that the trail will someday be part of a coordinated series of connected trails from the Florida Keys to Lake Champlain in upstate New York.

While Baker is quick to point out the importance of his friend Kegan's contributions to the project, Kegan is profuse in his praise of Baker. "Shad is a doggedly determined guy," Kegan said. "He's very organized and systematic and a good problem solver. He is ninety-nine percent responsible for the success of Pine Mountain Trail project."

Baker and Kegan share a common Christian faith, and Baker thinks it has been an influence on what has happened. "Ross and I committed this project to continual prayer, and we think God has had His hand in it all along the way."

Baker's tenacious and effective leadership, ignited when he realized that his own state of Kentucky offered nearby what he and friends had sought many miles away, has been the difference in the development of the Pine Mountain Trail at this juncture. The project promises to provide present and future generations a treasured look at the state's inspiring beauty and will provide increased recreational opportunities that will attract out-of-state tourists.

Shad Baker can take satisfaction in knowing that his vision will make Kentucky an even better place to live.

Billy Edwards

Cerebral Palsy Can't Derail Newspaper Columnist

His dark-haired and youthful appearance belies his early-fifties age. He nearly rivets out of his wheelchair with genuine excitement as he greets his visitor. His eyes are bright and joyful, his voice struggles with articulation, but a positive message—I'm happy and I'd love to tell you why—is communicated clearly. And though Henderson's Billy Edwards might have trouble speaking his message, his words in print may well bowl you over. They'll surely nudge you, even challenge you, to grow spiritually.

Edwards accepts the fact that he has cerebral palsy, that his limbs don't always do what he wants them to do, and that many people simply don't understand the words he speaks. What he can't accept is to see others around him not know of the love and strength that is available through personal faith in God.

That's why, since 1975, Edwards has worked from his home as a religious columnist for Henderson's newspaper, *The Gleaner*. The column, which appears in the Saturday edition of the newspaper, shows writing straight from the heart, practical for everyday living and written in a simple, readable style without being overly "preachy." He does his writing at a keyboard—punching out one key at a time. Edwards has the Billy Graham-like talent of taking relatively complex spiritual ideas and making them understandable to just about anyone. "And I didn't like writing in high school and I toughed it out in college. I just wasn't that creative," he said.

The "toughing it out in college" Edwards talked about is the time he spent at Middle Tennessee State University, in Murfreesboro, where he graduated in 1982 with a degree in mass communications with an emphasis in print journalism. Edwards, a native of Henderson, had moved to Murfreesboro in his childhood to receive special therapy not available near Henderson. He attended and graduated from Bellwood Christian Academy there before entering college at MTSU.

Billy Edwards

It was, as one might expect, a difficult task to handle the rigors of college life with his physical challenges. The school made appropriate adaptations for him though, and his determination was iron-clad. For Billy Edwards, MTSU was all good. "I loved it, and I thought I might just make a career of going to college there," he said with a laugh. "I used to stay on campus all day, sometimes from eight in the morning until almost midnight." As well as Edwards liked his college, appreciation for his accomplishment was showered upon him as he proudly guided his wheelchair across the stage to accept his diploma.

Ironically, Edwards and his strong faith commitment didn't join hands seriously until after his experience at Bellwood Christian Academy. "I couldn't get into religion then," he said. Gradually, his faith grew more important to him, starting while in college. Later, in 1985, Edwards became an ordained minister of the Baptist Church, though he did it without attending a seminary—a fact he doesn't seem to regret..

"The Lord has put me through the greatest school there is—the seminary of life," he said. "There are many things that any ministry must know about that a seminary can't teach you. They can't teach you compassion, or care, or how to care." Though you won't see Billy Edwards speaking from a pulpit on Sunday morning, he does his sermonizing through his *Gleaner* columns. He feels gratified when, through his word in print, "scales fall off of people's eyes and they see how much He (God) loves them, despite the kind of life they have lived in the past. It is the greatest experience you can have. This is what it's all about," he said.

Judy Jenkins, a features writer at *The Gleaner* and admirer of Edwards, knows how important he is to his readership. "They look so forward to his column," she said, "and knowing that it comes from Billy, who has had to overcome so many obstacles, it means more. He is one of the most gracious people I have ever known."

The Gleaner's editor, David Dixon, echoed the praise. "Billy Edwards' column has long been an important and popular element on the religion pages of *The Gleaner*. His columns are timely, accessible to readers and written with clarity," he said.

A true people person, Edwards enjoys the chance to spend time in the community of Henderson in his motorized wheelchair. Until recently, he worked as a Wal-Mart greeter, giving him a way of meeting his readers in person. When asked if not being as mobile as he'd like bothers him, his answer was both philosophical and upbeat. "Sure, everyone gets down no matter who you are, but the secret is that you don't stay down for the count! The Bible tells us that we are champions in Christ. He never told us that it would be easy."

Edwards gathers his column ideas in several ways, but ultimately, he said, they come "from the working of the Holy Spirit. At times I write from the frustrations of life. Sometimes I write from an idea that a reader may suggest. Very rarely do I go out into public without someone coming up to me and commenting about something I have written. We all need encouragement and this is how the Lord encourages me."

Dixon noted Edwards' special way of touching hearts. "Many of our readers know Billy beyond his efforts for *The Gleaner*. I'm sure they are truly inspired, both by his writing and by the courage and determination he displays in bringing those columns to them," Dixon said. "Those who might not know Billy personally still find inspiration in his reassuring weekly message."

Lee Jones

Bringing the Baseball 'RAP' to West Louisville

For 500 inner-city youths in Louisville, the term "RAP" has a different meaning than that of a trendy, cadenced music form. They're happily rapping out line drives and discovering the joy of balls, bats, bases and gloves—plus embracing a virtuous concept called teamwork. They're part of a summer baseball league called RAP, or Reaching All People, brainchild of a retired gentleman who didn't really retire at all.

When Lee Jones was growing up in Grenada, Mississippi, he learned some valuable lessons while playing baseball with his neighborhood buddies. "You didn't have to be tall like a basketball player of big like a football player to be good, so there was a place for everybody in the sport," he said.

That remembrance stirred Jones when, back in 1991 after retiring from management at Brown & Williamson Tobacco Company in Louisville, he noticed a couple of youths at a local park who were dominating the basketball court game because of their size and skills. The two didn't stop at that, however. "They taunted their teammates," Jones recalled. It looked to Jones like "they thought they didn't need each other and didn't need to use teamwork."

Concerned about that scene and sure it wasn't an uncommon occurrence, Jones met with some friends and suggested they do something about it—start a summer baseball league. His friends scoffed. "You will never get baseball in the Louisville inner-city. Basketball and football is too prominent here," they said.

Their words were a direct challenge to Lee Jones and his "can do" attitude. It fired his enthusiasm even more, and soon he convinced nine cohorts, some of whom worshiped with him at the Vonspigel Baptist Church, to meet for the purpose of developing a summer baseball league in Parkland in Louisville's West End.

Lee Jones

Jones's group initially encountered huge challenges, and it took seven months to get things up and running. "I walked around the area and there was grass up to my knees," he remembered. "At first, we had no monies. But pretty soon somebody donated a country-cured ham and we raffled it off for $1300. We pulled a trailer behind a truck to use for a concession stand. Then, the word got out and corporate America got involved (in the funding). David Jones, from Humana, gave us $700,000, along with others." Before long, four baseball fields were renovated. The first year, there were 100 youths involved, but as the organization began gaining momentum, the number jumped to 300, then 500—with over 200 parents involved on a daily basis. The formerly weedy and trashy parcel of earth—a magnet for undesirable behavior—today is the four million dollar Shawnee Sports Complex that spreads new hope for many who had already been going down the wrong paths early in life.

Looking back at the original group of nine who dreamed great things when they saw a need to help young people, Jones cited the standards they imposed on themselves. "We had strong criteria for ourselves. We agreed that if we were late for meeting three times without calling, we were out of the group. Or, if we missed twice, we were out." That set the stage for high expectancies in managing RAP. "We told adults that we wanted no drinking going on during the games," Jones said. "We expected ballplayers to have their shirts tucked inside their pants. And, we said that the only one allowed to wear their cap backwards was the one wearing shin guards and a face mask."

Jones's dedication was all consuming, especially for a supposedly "retired" person. "My wife told me I just ought to go over to that place and stay*,"* he said with a laugh. "I was working with RAP sixty to seventy hours per week."

But to Jones's glee, there was a strong effort coming from women to became part of the operation. "Women felt left out at first and they wanted to help. Mothers became a part of all aspects, and they took it just like a job," he said.

Jones sees clearly the obvious benefits that the baseball league has produced, such as decreased vice in the area, more meaningful life experiences for youth, and increased community involvement with their young. One of his greatest dreams is to see the youthful participants of RAP give back to their community as they grow into adulthood.

Jones spoke proudly of two college football stars who "came all the way through our program." They are University of Louisville player Michael Bush and University of Kentucky's Keenan Burton. "When U of L and Kentucky played this year, I just sat back and enjoyed it. I couldn't lose either way," he said with a smile. Jones sees the two as future NFL players who can someday be supportive, as former Baltimore Colt player Lenny Lyles already has, to improve even further the recent gains of the RAP program.

And though Lee Jones has won a goodly number of awards for his work, it's clear that the early training he received from his "very Christian parents" set a noble, purposeful path in front of him.

"They taught me to 'do everything without malice or envy,' to always do my very best," Jones said. "I am driven by my black race of people. We have adopted so many things that are not healthy for our culture."

In all his work for others, including his involvement with community endeavors outside RAP, Jones strives to model the best of his African-American heritage. "We are a loving people...always have been. We are a forgiving people. We've been a hard-working people. We dug all the ditches. We carried all the bricks on our shoulders to build buildings."

Jones is proud to say that all the funding for his three children's college education came from working another job—at a local hospital—while employed at Brown & Williamson. The three have all gone forward with successful careers.

Susan Rademacher, president of the local Olmstead Parks Conservancy, saw Jones's ideals and passion for helping the community at a meeting early in the program. "Lee's passion for the way baseball can mold children as team players, while nurturing their scholarship and citizenship, caught fire with children and parents alike," she said. "It was a vision of whole child, whole family, whole community that made the project to build the Shawnee Park Sports Complex so very special."

And don't forget about that little bit of Mississippi wisdom that caught fire in Lee Jones long ago. It was pretty special, too.

Martha Sparks

Voice of a Caregiver

Before Wilmore native Martha Evans married Bertel Sparks in 1952, she figured that her husband's Type I diabetes, the kind that children encounter, would be a concern, but not overly so.

In time, it was.

"Neither of us had any idea how this would color our lives," Martha said. "Bert told me later that if he had known how much work it would be, he wouldn't have married me—or anyone else." Today, because of their marriage and the wisdom gained from their time together, many are receiving help and comfort through Martha's spoken and written words.

Bert was a bright and successful lawyer who loved his profession. He, along with Martha, was active in church. During his career, he taught at New York University and Duke's law schools. He handled his medical condition with disciplined aplomb, sticking to a regimented diet usually prepared by Martha.

"Bert knew what he had to do, and he did it," Martha said. "There wasn't much leeway. We would eat together three times everyday, as he even came home from his office to eat lunch. For about thirty-five years of our marriage, he was mostly his own caregiver."

But an event that occurred earlier in adulthood came to bear on the couple's life—about thirty-five years later. "Bert was hit by a taxi in New York City. He suffered a concussion and a broken pelvis, but he seemed to heal from his injuries and went on with his life and work just fine," Martha said.

And except when he would have an occasional insulin reaction, which manifested symptoms similar to drunkenness, the years of their marriage and dealing with diabetes proved manageable, though time consuming. It also largely negated trips from home of any significant distance. "I do remember calculating that we did not venture farther than twenty-five miles from home for the last thirteen years of his life. The only exception was that I flew up to Kentucky from North Carolina for

Martha Sparks

my mother's funeral in 1981, and was gone two days. He stayed alone on that occasion," Sparks explained.

In 1988, Bert retired from nearly forty years of teaching law. About a year later, on a typical day while he was performing the routine task of taking a shower, he began to act strangely. "Bert got frustrated because he couldn't seem to get the water temperature properly adjusted. He called for me to help him with it, but he had actually emptied the hot water tank," Martha said.

It soon became known that Bert was exhibiting symptoms of dementia, probably originating long ago from the taxi accident in which waxy deposits accumulated on his brain. The condition, sadly, would plague him, and Martha, the rest of his life.

Now, with her husband's onset of debilitating dementia, Martha Sparks would make a dramatic change in her spousal role—going from Bert's helpmate to Bert's full-time caregiver. "Bert did so much to handle his diabetes himself, but now with the dementia, he was no longer capable," Martha explained.. She prepared his food, as always, but she had to decide if the amount was enough, or too much. She would have to make sure the timing for his meals was right. She relied on previous experience with Bert, but often had to rely on intuitive guesswork. Often, she guessed incorrectly, causing either insulin reactions or setting up the danger of blindness or kidney failure, among other conditions. Times were stressful, and even when she received occasional respite care, Martha was careful to instruct the helper that there was little margin for error in Bert's treatment. Hour after hour, day after day, Martha's focus was on Bert's needs. It was exhausting, and it was a mourning process. "You hate to see someone you love going to pieces...and unraveling," she said.

Throughout the period of full-time care giving, lasting about five years until he died in 1994, her patient was not demanding and did not level "guilt trips" toward Martha. "He never was like that," she said, "but it is not unusual for that to happen in those kinds of situations." During and after her care-giving experience, the bright and conscientious woman made mental notes and kept a journal. She began to recognize elements of care-giving that are common to many, but often not discussed. Feelings of emotional isolation, loss, unnecessary guilt, physical and emotional exhaustion, and anger are a few and, if she hadn't experienced all those emotions herself, she understood why other caregivers might. In the aftermath of taking care of her husband for many years, Martha Sparks hit on an important realization: "I feel like I learned a lot and it would be a shame not to share it with somebody."

Today, in her early eighties and quite energetic, Martha Evans Sparks is often called "America's Voice of the Caregiver." That's because she devotes her life to writing and speaking about care-giving. She hopes to inform, create understanding of the multi-faceted problems associated with care-giving, and, most of all, to be an encourager to the providers of such service.

A devout Presbyterian, Martha does it with a Christian perspective. She has written three books of spiritual meditations and advice on the subject of care-giving, and all are published by Wesleyan Publishing

House. Their titles are *Give Us This Day: Daily Hope for Caregivers, Cherish the Days: Inspiration and Insight for Long-Distance Caregivers and Strength for Today: Daily Encouragement Through Life's Transitions*. The books have been popular and have provided a wealth of positive response for their authenticity. She keeps a busy schedule of speaking engagements at churches and other group gatherings. Her web site, www.martha-evans-sparks.com, provides regular devotional lessons and an opportunity to give feedback. People often seek her out for advice or just to talk about care-giving.

Martha Sparks could have withdrawn and felt self-pity when her husband's medical condition worsened and the bulk of her life was centered on meeting his needs. She chose to take a more positive way, however, and in doing so, is helping many more people find perspective and hope in their own care-giving experience.

Jane Stephenson

Opening 'New Opportunities' to Women

When Jane Stephenson was growing up in the tiny mountain town of Banner Elk, North Carolina, she was painfully aware that girls, she explained, "were not allowed to do things boys did.

"We were not supposed to be smart," she said, "and because of that I got angry a lot. At ten-years-old, I guess I was part of early feminism."

She did have a unique advantage in living in Banner Elk, however, and it inspired her efforts to found the successful New Opportunity School for Women, first located in Berea, in 1987. NOSW's mission is to "to improve the educational, financial, and personal circumstances of low-come, middle-aged women of south-central Appalachia and Kentucky," and to date, over 500 women have benefited from the three-week residential program.

Banner Elk fortunately had a beacon of higher learning that made all the difference for Stephenson in those early years.

"Since Banner Elk had a small college, Lees-McRae, it opened up opportunities that many places in Appalachia didn't have," she said. "I took piano lessons from a college teacher, and I could check out books from the library." The college often had special programs in the arts that were enriching culturally for those in the community. "We were very fortunate to have options for learning that a lot of places in Appalachia didn't have."

Lees-McRae College served another vital purpose for Jane. She met John Stephenson, whom she later married. John was to become

Berea College's president, serving from 1984 until his death in 1994.

Photo by David Stephenson

"John had a deep interest in the study of Appalachia, and he used to ask me questions about it all the time," she said. "I remember when I was real young, a girl made fun of my accent, but I didn't even realize I was from Appalachia."

John accepted a teaching and administrative position at the University of Kentucky, and it was difficult for Jane to leave her native state. "I really didn't want to go to Kentucky at all," she said. She took courses at UK as she was raising three children, and in 1976 she

Jane Stephenson

received a master's degree in higher education administration. UK hired her to open a new office to advocate for non-traditional students, a group typically much older than other students. Their individual needs were challenging.

"Lots of them were divorced, with no money and going through transitions. They needed things like test-taking and study skills, so we provided them workshops to help," she said.

Just when things were getting settled in Jane's life, another family move occurred. John became Berea College's seventh president. She kept busy with duties related to John's position for a while, but one day got a call from noted Kentucky writer and friend Gurney Norman. He had a significant question for Jane.

"He wanted to know if Berea College had a program that could help a friend of his gain confidence, how to get a job, and improve her financial condition," she said. "She was experiencing an unexpected divorce and would soon have to support herself and two children."

A few days later, John was contacted by the Educational Foundation of America, in California, that had previously donated to Berea College for an innovative program. They asked President Stephenson if the school had any new and different programs that needed funding, and with a good proposal done promptly, they would consider funding it. That got the ball rolling, and Jane took control.

"I got on the phone to call together as many people on campus I could think of who could help design a program for women," she said. An enthusiastic brainstorming meeting in the Stephenson living room followed. Though not all questions were answered, wide support to use the college's resources was offered and soon a proposal was sent to the foundation. In December of 1986, the program was granted $14,000 per year for two years—exactly what the group requested. Jane soon was successful in receiving more funds from other individuals and small groups to start the project.

On June 7, 1987, twelve of the fourteen women selected for the inaugaral three-week program were in attendance. The schedule was packed and included: a tour of the library and the Appalachian Museum, an Appalachian literature course, a seminar on resource management, classes on job search skills, self-esteem, and computer basics. The group tapped into activities on campus such as author readings and folk dancing. "Weekends were spent touring Shakertown, Fort Boonesboro, and traveling to Lexington to a conference for women," Jane said, "and we held events for the families of the women on the day of graduation."

Today, after twenty years, the New Opportunity School for Women (NOSW) is still going strong. The organization conducts two three-week sessions per year in Berea and one in North Carolina, operating with annual budgets of $275,000 at Berea and $50,000 at Banner Elk. A total of 546 women have completed the sessions, along with several hundred others who have taken NOSW related, life-enhancing workshops. Of the graduates of the three-week sessions, seventy-five percent are now employed, twenty-seven have completed bachelor's degrees, with seven pursuing or achieving master's degrees. Many have received various certifications in professional fields.

The program that Gurney Norman hoped existed for his friend was created through Jane Stephenson's leadership and perseverance. The people who have gone through NOSW are full of gratitude. "I finally found myself and who I am," one graduate said, "living each day to the fullest and making my world a better place." In her 1995 book, *Courageous Paths: Stories of Nine Appalachian Women,* a sampling of graduates shared their own incredibly uphill life battles, who, with the support of NOSW, became over-comers. It inspired Norman to say, in the introduction: "If these women were ever at one time vulnerable to the manipulations of others, these narratives show that that time is now over."

Stephenson's NOSW hit another jackpot in recognition and fundraising in 2003 when she was selected as an "Oprah Angel" and won the "Use Your Life Award." The organization received $100,000 and Stephenson appeared on the Oprah Winfrey Show.

"Oprah came down into the audience to give me the award, give me a hug, and for me to thank her in a wobbly voice with tears in my eyes," Stephenson said. The NOSW website, which normally received about fifty hits per week, got 12,000 the week after the national TV appearance. The story of the program was now getting out there like no time before, and that would make the next progression doable.

Largely because of the vision of Stephenson, Frank Taylor and the $50,000 gift from the Kellogg Foundation, the program was expanded to the campus of Lees-McRae College at Banner Elk, starting in July of 2005. The Lees-McRae NOSW has since graduated thirty-three women and, says Stephenson, "is becoming known all over North Carolina."

People have asked Stephenson the question, "How can you possibly change a life in three weeks?" She has a ready answer.

"I can't tell you exactly but I can tell you that I have observed it happen, time after time, year after year" she said. "What we can all learn is that even a short-term intervention in a life can lead that person toward success."

Jane Stephenson started thinking that way when she was a ten-year-old growing up in Banner Elk. She never stopped.

Bennie Doggett

No Spirit of Fear

Bennie Doggett has always let others know where she stands on things of which she cares deeply. Being afraid isn't part of her makeup, so don't even bother to intimidate her.

"I just don't have a spirit of fear and never have," said Doggett, now in her mid-sixties and long a part of hard-driving social activism in her Covington community. Her work has not consisted of situations made for the meek at heart. She's encountered dangerous and violent people influenced by drugs, taken on bottom-line minded utility companies, fought hard to get jobs for the unemployed, and held hands with the dying. Through it all, she's made friends and a few enemies— and gained lots of respect.

Doggett has courage aplenty and an outrageous passion for helping those who struggle in life—those who are poor, who have addictions, who find themselves often in trouble with the law. Back in the 1980s, Doggett fought hard for her clients as the social-services coordinator for the Northern Kentucky Community Center. With the creativity and drive of a successful entrepreneur, she didn't wait for those she served to come to her first, however. Her clientele was built largely by handing out business cards to just about anybody in the area who looked like they needed some help. And the clients came. In a 1987 article in *The Kentucky Post*, it stated, "Ms. Doggett deals with about 6,500 emergency cases each year and counsels 4,500 clients a year. A lot of 'Miss Bennie's' work is conducted outside of her wide-windowed office... She recently moved close to the center. 'If they see my window open, they come over to talk,' she said."

Doggett will probably not be widely known for her skills of diplomacy, at least not those exemplified in her early years of work. In frustration, she once called the Public Utility Commission in Frankfort regarding a local mother and her eleven children who had their electricity turned off. She threatened to call television cameramen to photograph the shivering family if the electricity was not turned on. Her

Bennie Doggett

persistence paid off, though she realizes now that her methods needed to mellow a bit. "I was not trained in college with a degree in social work," she admitted. "I received my training from life experiences." Many of those experiences came from growing up poor in Cincinnati's West End, where as a child little Bennie taught her father to read and followed her mother's example of helping the poor and uneducated around her neighborhood.

A small sampling of her duties as a long-time, pro-active force in her Covington neighborhood reads like this: taking clients to the hospital, helping illiterate clients fill out food stamp forms, making sure senior citizens get their free government commodities, and counseling young delinquents to change their ways.

While spending many long, hard hours at the center, Doggett, who is a sharp, even dazzling dresser, also opened her own business—a women's clothing store downtown called Personal Touch. "Not bragging, but God gave me a talent for being creative and being a good organizer," she said. Her business did well, and she kept it going for fourteen years. That is, until so many people came to her for help and advice about daily problems. This was added to the fact that her sister became ill with cancer. As always, Bennie Doggett wouldn't turn a person down who needed her. She spent a year and a half as her sister's caregiver before she died. Doggett then became an outreach worker for Covington's Eastside while working through the Community Action Center.

Doggett then decided to retire from doing social work, but that didn't last long. She joined and became an active member of the Ninth Street Baptist Church, and a new challenge developed for her. "I came out of retirement," Doggett said, "to volunteer thirty-two hours per week at the Oasis Outreach Center." She's still working there, even as she is caring for an ill relative.

The Oasis Outreach Center is a ministry created by her church to provide programs that, according to the church's web site, "...deter community deterioration, by promoting self-sufficiency and continued improvements through education, support, guidance, employment and assisted living." So far, Doggett said, the Center "has been a blessing. We want to claim back this corner." Formerly located at the Ninth Street Baptist Church, it now sits proudly at 1016 Greenup Street, formerly a dangerous place of crime and drug abuse. It has an attractive building that is filled with donated, but nice, equipment and furniture. People are having their needs met, and one can sense that Bennie Doggett is "feeling it" again.

"We stepped out on faith on the center," she explained. "We're able to help assist people on their mortgages and rent and give some food assistance through vouchers. We have about twenty volunteers all together, and we're able to help with some job training and with those who are homeless." Good stuff and Bennie Doggett-style, indeed.

Dan Hassert, managing editor of the *Kentucky Post* and a native of Covington, knows well of Doggett's work. The newspaper has followed her influence in Covington for years. "Bennie Doggett has spent a lifetime being a sort of untrained social worker, lawyer and ombudswoman/problem solver for poor people in Covington's African-

American Eastside neighborhood. She's a gem, a fighter and stubborn."

Bennie Doggett is never one to mess with when she's fighting for disadvantaged people, something she started doing as a child.

George and Mary Jo Phillips

A Lifetime of Ministry

When George and Mary Jo Phillips began their marriage in the 1950's, the bride proclaimed that she wanted to be "the most perfect preacher's wife I could be." She meant it, but if she had foreseen the future of their life in ministry, she might have been more than a little nervous.

Now, after over fifty years in partnership, the couple will tell you it hasn't been an easy road. But they will tell you it has been an adventurous, joyous, and fulfilling one. Together, they have shared their unconditional and unconventional love for literally thousands of needy "souls," including young people from broken or dysfunctional homes, alcoholics and illicit drug users, the poor and the uneducated.

Affiliated with the United Methodist Church, the two led local ministries at large churches and tiny ones, located in places like downtown Louisville and very rural, sparsely populated Island, Kentucky. Later, Mary Jo supported George's full-time evangelistic endeavor as he preached throughout the United States and many foreign countries while she "kept the home fires burning," taking care of their four children. They are still busy and serving today, spry and energetic though in their seventies.

George is the pastor at the Beech Creek United Methodist Church in Greenville, in Muhlenberg County, and Mary Jo shares her musical talents and passion for young people there. On Tuesday nights, George teaches a class for those who have a chemical dependency problem and are ordered by the local drug court to attend. Many participants are making positive changes, including to seek church membership at Beech Creek.

To the myriad of things the two have accomplished, George continually refrains, "To God be the glory. It has been a wonderful life for us."

In a strong and forthright Southern voice, George spoke of his background. "I was born in the backwoods of southern Mississippi, thirty miles south of Jackson. I was one of six children, and my father was a poor dirt farmer. There were two things he wanted us to do, become a Christian and get an education. He didn't have a penny to help us, but five of us got college educations, and three got master's degrees."

Photo: Studio III Photography

George and Mary Jo Phillips

For George Phillips, his foray into college was on pure faith. "I hitchhiked thirty miles to Milsaps College, affiliated with the United Methodist Churches, stood in line and registered for classes," he recalled. When it came time to pay, young Phillips told them he had no money and hoped that since he had been licensed, at age fifteen, to preach in their churches, he thought they should help him get his education at the school. Taken by surprise, the school nonetheless found some scholarship money and a few jobs, and allowed him to attend the college. The administration's confidence was rewarded as George thrived there. The mature youngster even preached at a local church during the period.

George and Mary Jo married in 1951. George entered Vanderbilt University to work on his master's degree in church history and counseling. During that time, he also was hired to preach at a Cumberland Presbyterian church near Nashville. After receiving the degree, he and Mary Jo held ministries at several small churches in Mississippi before moving to Island, Kentucky, in 1957 to pastor another church.. They were afforded numerous challenges in this poor, west Kentucky coal mining area in McLean County. First, the community widely suffered from lack of education. "The mean grade level for the people around Island was fifth or sixth grade," George said. "They needed a principal at the Island Elementary School, and since I was about the only one who had enough education to get an emergency certificate, they asked me to take the job for a year." Though it was tough simultaneously leading a church congregation and also a school, it was also fertile grounds to embrace the couple's passion for youth.

"We have always emphasized young people in our ministries," said George. "We always start with getting the youth interested in church first, then get the parents to follow." At the Island United Methodist Church, there were about ten young people involved when the Phillips' couple came. In two years, the gathering had grown to about a hundred.

"We started encouraging them to go to college, which was almost unheard of around the Island community," George said. "If they didn't have enough money for college, we tried to raise it or find some for them." They count as many as seventeen took the college challenge, and George and Mary Jo are proud to say some have become ministers, some became successful in the corporate world, and many simply took advantage of a new world of opportunities in their daily lives that the education afforded them.

The couple later held ministries at Campbellsville and Louisville. At the Broadway United Methodist Church in Louisville, there were about fourteen youths involved when the two arrived. It grew in seven years to over 200, and the group, under direction of the Phillips' was involved heavily in evangelism in places like Cherokee Park and downtown Louisville during late hours. "We put our kids on the bus, and with adult supervision, we let them witness on streets and in the park," George said.

Besides reaching out to the youth wherever their desire to serve God leads them, the two have always established an anti-alcohol component in each church where they labored. "As a boy growing up, my grandmother kept me away from my grandfather because he was an alcoholic. She didn't want us kids to be around it," George said. His grandmother's influence is still strong today, and George makes it clear he was, and is, on a mission concerning the problem of abusive drinking. "God called me to minister to alcoholics, and lots of people have been set free because of it. To God be the glory," he proclaimed with his humble, yet typical, air of certitude.

Today, the couple actively involve themselves in a similar kind of service at the Beech Grove United Methodist Church in Greenville, near their home of Central City. George is the pastor, Mary Jo works with the youth, and on Tuesday nights George leads classes on drug abuse. Many of his students' children have become involved with the church, as well as some parents. "We have had over eighty people attend three or more sessions in the three years we have done this," George said. "Our success rate is better than A.A. Some have been led to Christ through the program."

Though George Phillips has often spearheaded the projects that he an Mary Jo collaborated to implement, the development of a day care center in Asuncion, Paraguay, in South America, can be largely associated with her leadership. In the process of supporting the growth of churches in the poorest areas of Paraguay, a need arose for a way to allow poor mothers to work for subsistence. She obtained financing for the purchase of a building lot for a day-care center by selling labeled drinking cups and a small booklet containing a compilation of her writings in a newsletter sent to George's evangelistic association.

"I never dreamed that those two items would sell like that," Mary Jo said. "I was really excited that they were able to have a daycare center there. I love children and wanted to help." George told of Mary Jo's admirers who lived in the area. "They named the facility after her.

They thought so much of her that mothers would line up just to have her hold their babies."

No one would blame the two, after such a service-oriented life, to take a rest. George and Mary Jo Phillips could be spending their days coasting along, enjoying the fruits of their legacy of faith, feeling a sense of contentment. But, despite some recent health concerns for Mary Jo, the couple retain their deep desire to share their love and faith. They have been blessed by a network of loving friends gained over years of service to others. It emboldens them, and as long as they are able, one can figure they will continue to serve and say, together: "To God be the glory."

Beulah Hester

Throwing Herself into a Life of Perseverance

As a youngster in Mercer County, Glen Hughes's McAfee School team played against her. She was the only girl on Cornishville School's seventh and eighth grade softball squad, in fact, the only girl on any squad they played against.

There was something golden about her. "I marveled at her throwing arm. It was the best on their team," he said. Interestingly, the small-town, female diamond ace later made a much bigger pitch in her life. She developed a talent to do creative sewing, then used her connection to ball-playing, and particularly to the game's umpires, to start a business that became a national leader in the sales of umpire attire.

The events that got her to that point are riveting. Her sparkling success came after a remarkable story of old-fashioned and stubborn perseverance. But the stirring account of her life actually started many years before she played her first game with the boys.

It was a cold November day at Grandma's house in Harrodsburg. The grandchildren were playing in the way most kids played in 1951, without TV video games or other electrical gadgets to distract them from each other. Seven-year-old Beulah Carr had done what her mother had told her; she would need to leave her snowsuit pants on, but she could remove the top part since it was warm inside. Meanwhile, on the stove near where Beulah lay on the floor, a boiling kettle of water was beginning to dance. Within seconds, the unthinkable happened. Little Beulah instinctively arose, screaming, just as the kettle and its contents fell towards her vulnerable, thin body—giving her the full shot on her back and right arm.

"Grandma put hot tea leaves on the burns," said Beulah Hester, fifty-six years later. "In those days, they always put heat on to treat burns." Beulah's mother rushed her to the hospital, where doctors gave her even odds to survive her third degree burns. Even if she did live, they said, Beulah might lose the use of her right arm. Stringent exercising of the arm would be needed almost daily. She survived her critical

Beulah Carr Hester

injuries, and fifteen days later she was at her rural Mercer County home, convalescing in her special "tent bed," which meant that a piece of cloth material hung above her body in tent-like fashion, furnishing her with added heat for her wounds. The child continued to suffer grueling pain, however.

"Mom had to put hot salt water on towels and put on my back in order to take dead skin off. I remember how bad it hurt," Hester said. She missed forty days of her second grade year at tiny, two-roomed Bohon School, where people like her teacher and bus driver, as well as her classmates, nursed her along with loving compassion.

When Beulah was ready to begin physical recovery, her father played a big role. "I started throwing a ball every day to Dad," she said. "We started the summer after the accident, and he bragged on how I threw." In the next few years, she gained strength—and ball playing skill. The neighborhood kids began to gather for games and Beulah more than held her own in talent level. By the time she was in the eighth grade at Cornishville School, she was allowed to play on the boys' softball team. Her experience, skills, and love for the sport motivated her to play later, after high school, in some industrial leagues around the area.

But the sport's greatest impact on her life, and career, would come in the future.

After high school, Hester started work at Cricketeer Manufacturing, a sewing factory in Harrodsburg. She had a knack for sewing; was even quite creative about it, and took an interest in learning as many different jobs at the plant as she could. In about four years, she became a salaried supervisor and started a family and moved to Stanford. With the time factor and rigors of her job, plus being married and raising three children—one who suffered from a serious asthmatic condition— any extra softball playing ceased. "I dedicated myself to be the best I could for my family," she said.

In 1985, a dispute with management in which Hester thought another employee was treated unfairly motivated her to resign and start her own sewing-alteration business in downtown Danville. She attracted enough customers to soften the blow of leaving the sewing factory, but in her own home a storm was brewing.

Her husband, Don, well respected and president of the country club in Stanford, began to act strangely. "He started saying things that didn't make sense," Hester said, "and others at the country club noticed it, too." A doctor first mentioned that he "acted like an alcoholic," but later tests showed that he had developed a serious brain tumor. Surgery to remove the growth was performed, and he improved considerably— for a while. At that point, Hester moved her sewing alteration business into the family garage in Stanford to give more attention to the challenges. But in 1991 Don's tumor returned, and he died in 1992. Beulah's persevering spirit, honed early in her life as she handled the accident that nearly took her own life, was now being tested again. She was now a single mother with three children and a whole lot of financial stress. She continued to do alterations in her home, but she also took a position with the local high school day care center for a year. "It was a job I didn't care for at all," she said, "but I needed the health insurance."

During that period, Hester gained some valuable information from a friend. "One of the ladies at my church also worked at the National Softball Association (NSA) in Nicholasville," she said, "and an official there wanted to find a more useful and better quality ball bag for their umpires."

With that challenge planted in Beulah Hester's mind—and with her ball playing interest and natural ability in sewing matters—she got busy. "I had been mowing the yard, and sat down to rest a while when a solution for the ball bag hit me," she explained. She quickly put together the bag she envisioned and delivered it to her NSA connection. It was an immediate hit, and NSA ordered thirteen bags for a tournament their umpires were working. She completed training in the art of embroidery and soon acquired a patent on her special umpire bag. NSA became a regular buyer of bags and other accessories, and soon other customers came.

It was a good start, but her fledgling enterprise located in her garage hit a home run in 1997. "I discovered the internet," she said. Hester's company was named Ump-Attire, and with it's web site advertising her unique and quality umpire clothing and accessories to an international market, her business took off. The success of Beulah Hester's entrepreneurship resulted in articles in *Referee Magazine*, *The Lane Report*, the *Lexington Herald-Leader*, and a mention in the *Wall Street Journal*. The little seven-year-old Mercer County girl who suffered critical burns had made a remarkable comeback.

But even with Ump-Attire drawing attention as one of the leading national companies in its sales niche, Hester dealt bravely with a variety of family concerns. Her mother battled a stroke suffered in 1997 that left her paralyzed and her father received a diagnosis of lung cancer and was admitted to a nursing home in 1999. Both her parents died in 2000. Hester's asthmatic daughter continued to require hospital treatment. She died in 2004.

Some bad luck in several decisions regarding her business created some obstacles as the 21st century unfolded, but for Hester, her never quit attitude has put her back in the winner's circle again. That shouldn't be a surprise, because in her life of perseverance, The Girl with the Golden Arm has often gotten two strikes, but she's never struck out.

Russell Vassallo

Animal Rescuer Finds Personal Peace

It was the year 2000, and the dark clouds of chronic depression hovered around Russell Vassallo.

It was understandable, for the sixty-six-year-old New Jersey native had experienced a lot of the distasteful in his life. When he was only eighteen months old, a mastoid infection almost killed him, and it affected his hearing. He had bronchial pneumonia, probably caused by severe allergies, and he spent long hours by himself, often in the third floor bedroom of his family's house where he felt isolated. He was very short (only five feet, two inches today), and he was often rejected by other children in his Newark neighborhood.

As Vassallo grew older, the positive things in his life were more than interspersed with hard-hitting difficulties. He was thrown out of two high schools for insubordination. In adulthood, he had marriage problems with his first wife and trying times with his children. He was thrown from a horse and suffered a broken hip and ribs. He again came close to death with advanced colon cancer. A graduate of Seton Hall School of Law, he nearly came to fisticuffs several times in his prosperous, but tumultuous, career as a trial lawyer. "I always thought of myself as strong-willed, and I had a lot of anger inside me," he said.

But as Vassallo gazed ahead at a new millennium while living in his transplanted home in rural Casey County, a 224 acre farm, he was tired of doing things the old way. Instead of placing emphasis on medicine for his depression, he began to spend more time opening himself up to what he calls his "animal friends"—a love he had developed long ago as the isolated, sickly child who spent a lot of time in his third floor room. "I remember about the only fun I had in those days was being allowed to go outside and play for about an hour with my little Pomeranian dog, Palsy," he recalled.

Vassallo mentally set himself on a path to conquer his sometimes undisciplined anger. In that regard, Vassallo began to pour out his

Russell Vassallo

thoughts and feelings on paper. He became a motivated writer with laser focus. His writing was something he had toyed with all his life, but never with such intensity. His topic, almost exclusively, was about animals he and his second wife, Virginia, had rescued and raised on their farm outside the Kentucky town of Liberty.

Today, in his seventies, Vassallo has settled into a busy, productive life as a published author and speaker, a small-time farmer, and along with his wife, an animal rescuer who spends about $14,000 per year in out-of-pocket expenses for the on-going project.

His first book, *Tears and Tales*: *Stories of Animal and Human Rescue*, is a series of short stories revolving around his animal friends. It has been popular, and his second book, *The Horse with the Golden Mane*, has also done well. Though the books are technically fictionalized, the stories are based on true relationships forged with a multitude of animals under the care of Vassallo and his wife. Throughout his writings, the often complex links between human to animal interaction are explored through personal anecdotes and revealing, visceral observations. For Vassallo, his insights are both perceptive and highly intuitive. He writes with rare transparency and courage; his personal struggles and insecurities—as well as his deeply compassionate, sensitive nature—are generously on display.

At book festivals and writing conferences, Vassallo is sought out by patrons who share his passion. Speaking to groups, his personal accounts are riveting; they touch people emotionally. In describing *Tears and Tales*, Vassallo is succinct and open. "It's about me, my wife, my animal friends," he said. "It's about the hopes and dreams of every man and woman who loves and needs to be loved. It's about not letting go and sometimes having to let go. It's about laughing and crying and wanting to return to read, to laugh, to cry again. Now I've spoken my piece and the voice within me is still."

On a recent summer morning, Vassallo guided this writer around his Winter Hills Farm and introduced him to his "friends." The first meeting was with Red Leader, called "Red," a fifteen-year-old fit and beautiful horse who wore a dark fly mask over his eyes. "Red came from the New Jersey Standardbred Association and had won $100,000," said Vassallo. "He had fractured a bone in his leg, and they kept racing him. He broke down totally." The Vassallos acquired Red seven years ago, and previous inhumane treatment was clear. "It took a long time for me to calm him down. He won't let anyone but me ride him," Vassallo said.

While the writer watched, Red Leader engaged in playful behavior, both jumping around and rolling on the grass, behaviors which Vassallo said were "showing off to the visitor."

Then two blackish-colored dogs, Spunky and Sweetpea, wiggled their way toward the visitor. "Spunky is part Sharpei and part pit bull," Vassallo said, "and Sweetpea was in one of my stories, and I called him 'Git.' He showed up wretched looking because somebody had taken his pups away."

Another canine recently appeared with a collar, and it was returned to its owners, then tried to return to the Vassallos. Also finding sanctuary on the farm were five other horses: Diablo and Uno (a father-son), Lonesome Day, Dusty Dart, and Power Blaster, known through Vassallo's writing as "Taj."

Vassallo talked about two types of cats that are part of the non-profit operation. "We have three barn cats, one of whom, Spooky, recently came up crippled so we are nursing her in our basement," he said. The Vassallos put Spooky under a vet's care, who recommended "putting it down," usually a no-no for Vassallo. "We spent about $1000 on Spunky, who's doing better but can't walk straight. We also have two indoor cats, Boots, whom we rescued on the road, and Sassy, who was the runt of the litter and had to find a home or be destroyed."

Though not all of the animals are still around, the Vassallos figure Virginia and him have rescued about eighteen animals in the last fifteen years, even more if one goes way back in time. "As a child one of my grandfather's dogs bit me behind the ear," Vassallo said, "and my grandfather, an old Italian who loved his namesake, wanted to shoot the dog, but I clung to Queenie's neck and wouldn't let go. He had to forego his plans to kill the dog. I was five then."

But these days, the short-in-stature Vassallo casts a broadening shadow of influence in his desire to help both his animal and human friends who struggle with difficult challenges. His books are selling. His requests to speak are becoming more common. Driving his internal engine is a deep and abiding sense of gratitude for the often uncondi-tional love shown him by his animal friends and fellow humans. Many souls are almost magically connected by his brave willingness to lay open his heart, part and parcel, for all to see.

His wife Virginia, wholly a part of Russ Vassallo's graciousness, talked about observing him as he writes his stories. "Sometimes he just cries as he is putting the words down on paper," she said, "and then when he reads them. He's very emotional about it."

That's because Russell Vassallo has said his piece…and now he *has* peace.

Fr. John Rausch

Fighting for the Poor and Conservation of the Land

"Everyone should have enough... to *be* more."

At first, one might scratch their head at that statement. Odd, simplistic, possibly cryptic in nature. But for Fr. John Rausch, who spoke the words, his elaboration began to bring a little clarity to the writer on a cold, January day while the priest served soup and sandwich to his guest.

"Think about it," he said. "If you were sitting there thinking about your hunger pangs and where you were going to eat later, you and I wouldn't have a very good exchange here, would we?" Fr. Rausch extended the thought. "Having *enough* frees people to achieve more, to be more. The market system always rewards the strongest, the smartest. What happens when someone is not smart, they're aged, they're not so good looking? Because people are created in the image of God, they all deserve to have enough. Enough food, adequate housing and good healthcare, so they don't have to worry about those things. Then they can be more."

The Stanton priest, dressed in blue jeans and a flannel shirt sans religious collar, spoke in an even, deliberate voice. He moved on to the subject of protecting "God's beauty of creation"—the land. He talked of eastern Kentucky's disappearing mountaintops (as coal is extracted after basically removing the summits from selected mountains) and the residual, negative effects on its Appalachian people.

"At McRoberts, in Letcher County, there had only been one major flood since 1957. Because of mountaintop removal, since the year 2000 there have been five major floods," stated Rausch.

Photo by Jean Bach

As the conversation continued over a fine meal (Fr. Rausch is a gourmet cook), the writer developed the sense that the priest's love of the common folk, the appreciation for the landscape, and a perception of eastern Kentucky's needs are paramount in his thought process. Rausch exudes hope, an apparently undying belief that people can "come together" and make the world better.

Fr. John Rausch

Using his platform as the coordinator of the Office of Peace and Justice for the Diocese of Lexington and the director of the Catholic Committee on Appalachia, plus being a card carrying priest in the Glenmary society, Fr. Rausch challenges his Catholic brethren, and others who would listen, to look out for the needs of those who are shut out from resources taken for granted by many in America. He promotes discussions as he educates and cajoles his audiences about the need to take better care of our earth. He does so by adapting a dignified respect for the ones who disagree with him, by looking for commonality in goals, and using a variety of ways to deliver the message. Rausch has been called by journalist Jean Sammon "a prophet in Appalachia." Sammon, writing for a Catholic social justice organization, *NETWORK,* said "Though he lives, works and thinks in Kentucky, his thoughts reach a global audience through his writings and workshops."

A Philadelphia native, Rausch, was transplanted via the Catholic Church into the Appalachian area of Kentucky over thirty years ago.

He has stayed, growing more passionate about the people, the culture, and the geography—despite the chronic obstacles the region faces: poverty, lack of good job opportunities, low school achievement and environmental concerns. He has used his master's degree in economics as a credible background to teach his passion. In his writings as a columnist, or talking to groups or individuals, Rausch offers his dreams for the area's future. "We can improve our economy and help our people have more choices. I would like to see more communal type places. Places where people live closer and help each other out. I hope to see a cleaner environment. Appalachia could become a place of spiritual rebirth, where there is a renewal of common sense and a decent way to live," he said.

Rausch gives regular tours of eastern Kentucky, often as many as five per year. Typically, about fifteen individuals travel with Rausch as they make visits to such diverse sites as Eula Hall's Mud Creek Clinic, which accepts medical patients regardless of their ability to pay, or the David School, a school where young people with limited financial resources and a need for alternative educational practices can succeed. The Rausch convoy might be spotted near a mountain scarred by questionable mining practices, or where frequent flooding has occurred. Rausch may lead a group to a small herb farm, or to a craft shop, or maybe even to a small, Catholic church along the way.

His aim is to provide authentic awareness of modern mountain life in Kentucky, and that includes both the good and the bad. "At the end of the day, I ask my guests questions like 'What did you see? How does this fit what you expected to see?' Many come from other parts of the country," said Rausch, "and they take back home some ideas they can use. I view many economic problems of Appalachia as a microcosm of the whole country."

Rausch talked about one tangible result of the leadership effort. "A strong Republican, a real conservative, went along on one of our tours. When I asked for an evaluation, he asked to think about it and get back with me later. When he did, he told me he was changing his platform in regard to solving some specific problems here. He felt now like there was a way for the government to be of help."

Rausch's writings frequently confront issues of worldwide debate: the bloodletting in Darfur, global warming and the easy accessibility of guns as a strong factor in violence in America. Economic justice appears on the agenda continually, especially as it affects people's behavior and sense of pride. In a recent column, he noted that "the widening income gap leaves those left behind feeling like losers." Rausch is straightforward, but dignified and respectful, in railing against corporate exploitation and the waste of the world's resources.

Wherever Fr. Rausch speaks, he stresses the essentiality of relationships, or true community. He frequently sends verbal zingers to his audience, typically designed to make people think harder and to examine entrenched notions, such as the adage "pulling oneself up by their bootstraps." Rausch answers by stating, "There is no such thing as a self-made man. All profit is social profit. One must have the help of others to succeed economically."

In a recent column, the priest decried the use of bottled water worldwide, where the empties have become an environmental concern. Noting both the healthiness of drinking water and the profit involved, he remarked that he would be "pilloried from both the left and right." He has been regularly criticized by coal company executives who aren't happy with Rausch's stand against mountaintop removal. After one Pike official made it clear he didn't think Rausch knew what he was talking about, the priest suggested a meeting to talk about the issues involved. "The first time we met, things didn't go well between our two groups," Rausch said, "so when we met again and I hired a mediator to moderate the meeting. It went better, and, in the end, we agreed to disagree. Now, every time I go down to Pikeville to speak, I'm received well even though not everyone agrees on issues. We can get things done when there is good feeling toward each other. That's the power of human relationships."

As a Glenmary priest, of which Rausch is one of about sixty members, his objective is to show, and help offer, the Catholic faith in small towns around eastern Kentucky where there has not previously been a large presence. Through his work for the Office of Peace and Justice, he speaks "about thirty-five times per year in the Lexington Diocese, where I can say things that the church's regular priest might find uncomfortable to say." He is highly sought after as a speaker. He was given 2007 Pax Christi USA "Teacher of the Year Award," and his insights on social and environmental issues are often quoted in Catholic and secular publications.

Father John Rausch's message to uplift the people and land of eastern Kentucky and beyond marches on, despite angering many with opposing political viewpoints. He passionately preaches his message from the barren mountaintops—and the flooded valleys. Carefully, patiently, articulately, and continually, the good priest paints insightful word pictures and acts as an individual model of a world he sees where all will be treated with wholly dignified respect, and the land they trod is deliberately and lovingly tended.

Della Jones

Teacher's Spirit, Perseverance Outlast Racism and Sexism

Williamstown's Della Jones has experienced more history than many of us have studied in books. When she was born on July 7, 1903, women in the U.S. didn't have the right to vote. World War I was still more than a decade away. Her own African-American race, still suffering from the remnants of slavery, was treated as second-class citizens. There were no television sets, no commercial airplane flights and no modern air conditioning to make homes more comfortable.

But, times have changed, and Jones is a true witness of the fact. And, for Jones, much of her perspective comes from the lenses of being a professional educator in Kentucky's public schools.

In 1922, Jones graduated from the noted Lincoln Institute, a high school for blacks in Shelby County. The school's president, Whitney Young, was the father of national civil rights activist and National Urban League director, Whitney Young, Jr., who Della Jones "held as a baby in my hands many times."

She realized early that she wanted to be a teacher. At age nineteen, she passed an exam that allowed her to gain a teaching position in rural Wayne County. "I finished the school term there, about three months. It was grades one to eight, and I had twenty-nine students all together. Then I went to Kentucky State College, in Frankfort (now Kentucky State University) to summer school and got a teaching certificate that would be good for four years."

Jones parlayed her new teaching certificate into a position at an all-black school in rural Boone County, near Burlington. "It was a good teaching experience," she said, "and there were very few discipline problems. I can't understand how today there are so many."

Along about the time her four-year certificate expired, Jones got married and decided to take a break from being an educator for a while. However, her hiatus from teaching lasted much longer than expected. "In 1929, the state legislature passed a law that married women could not teach, " she said, "and I was out of teaching for thirteen years. I had always wanted to go back to college and get my degree, though."

Photo courtesy of Grant County News

Della Jones

The law concerning married women in education was changed, and Jones soon resumed her teaching career, this time in a small school in the small town of New Liberty, in Owen County. Dividing her residences between there and her home in Williamstown, she had to travel a circuitous path to her job "every month or two." Jones reminisced about her challenge in getting to work, "I first had to go to Walton to catch a train to Worthville. Then I would stay all night there, get up early and ride a mail bus to New Liberty."

Her dream of a college degree continued to be intense, so late into her thirties, the determined Jones returned to KSU to take summer classes. Besides doing correspondence and some extension work at Georgetown College, Jones attended summer school at Kentucky State for an amazing seventeen years. In the early summers, she "put my little girl in a training school while I was in classes there." Finally, in 1957, Della Jones proudly accepted her bachelor's degree diploma in education from Kentucky State in Frankfort—and heard an inspirational commencement address from a relatively unknown young civil rights activist and minister by the name of Martin Luther King, Jr.

In the late 1950s, Jones became a librarian at a northern Kentucky high school which was by now racially integrated. When pressed to talk about any experiences of racism directed toward her, the gracious centurion remarked, "I don't like to say bad things about people, but I had a principal who was as biased as could be."

She recalled a Shakespearean play performance at the school. Teachers were allowed to attend, but the principal directed her to "go back to the library where you can supervise the students who didn't go to the play." When Jones returned to the library, she found there were no students not attending the performance. That, along with many other instances of the principal's abuse, ripened things to a head on one particular day. "Some students of mine saw how the principal was treating me, and they actually booed him. In time, he did soften some, but not too much," she said.

Della Jones made a lot of friends in her over thirty-seven years in the education profession. Though wheelchair bound, the 103-year-old lives by herself in the home in Williamstown where her parents raised her. Her husband died in 1969. She is an avid fan of the Kentucky Wildcats basketball team, and her small house's walls are adorned with many photos, including one with former UK basketball coach Tubby Smith. She seldom misses a game on TV. She often gets special visitors, too. "I have a lot of wonderful friends," she said, eyes sparkling, "and my students come by and bring their grandchildren. I was a dedicated teacher."

Few would doubt Della Jones's dedication. She has a long, long legacy of history to prove it.

Doug Corbin

Extending Love from the Appalachians
to the Mountains of Honduras

Dozens of small photographs lay spread across the middle-aged man's kitchen table. Nearly all were images of Latin American natives, sun-kissed and rural, looking of the most modest means. The man, with traces of emotion, gently held the photographs in his rough-hewn hands, treating his visitor to moments of fond reflections and telling what his friends are like. It was a tender, compassionate telling, a bit unusual for a male raised during the often stoic "greatest generation." One could rightly surmise that the sharing time could last indefinitely, if needed. For sure, it was clear the man knew the people, and they him.

Doug Corbin's adoration for the people of Honduras started in 1992 when Rev. Tom Hockaday, a local Methodist pastor, wrote in the local newspaper column about his mission trip there. The minister's words stirred the humble and devout Russell County resident to use his resources and talents to help make a better life for the desperately poor of Honduras and, while there, to "harvest souls for our Lord and Christ" Today, in his late fifties, he is unwavering and persevering in his goals to serve.

Since 1992, Corbin has made at least sixteen trips to the northern country in Central America, where his selfless acts of love are making a significant, lasting difference. Always, he has raised his own finances along with the support of his church congregation, Jamestown Nazarene Church.. He would prefer, rather, to say "the Lord provided me." With near child-like faith, Doug Corbin is a man who appears to be guided every moment by his religious faith—along with the experiences of his own past.

His passion for the disadvantaged started welling up deep inside him many years before. In 1958, living in the White Oak Creek area in Adair County with two brothers and a sister, eight-year-old Doug Corbin and his siblings were uprooted from their family when their

Doug Corbin

parents divorced. "My grandparents gave word to my father that the children would be taken from the home and split up," Corbin recalled. "One day we were taken to my grandparents by my father. It was unusual, but we ended up staying there that night. At two o'clock in the morning, we were awakened and we traveled all of the next day. We ended up at the Grundy Mountain Mission School in Grundy, Virginia."

Though not happy about leaving their home, the children were treated with compassion at the mission. "I learned many years later that it was the only thing my father could do to keep the kids together," Corbin said.

Years passed, and as an adult, Corbin settled in the Russell County area, where he married and raised three children while farming and working an assortment of jobs around the region. His childhood raised in an orphanage was indelibly imprinted in his mental make-up, and Corbin was inspired to lend a loving, understanding hand to others experiencing distress. When the opportunity presented itself, he eagerly made contact with Hockaday, a Methodist minister, regarding his wishes to help with the ministry in Honduras.

Corbin soon put aside enough money to go to Honduras for two weeks to help on a project "almost two miles up into the mountains." His task was a bit unusual. Corbin's group introduced the growing and processing of sorghum molasses to a population that suffered perpetually from malnourishment. They encountered difficulties when it came to straining the molasses juice, mainly because of the lack of resources available in the area. "We didn't have a large container to put the cane juices in," Corbin said, "and someone brought a small cup that we put some of the cane juice in. Some of the Hondurans took the green colored juice and drank it because it was so sweet and something they didn't normally get to have. We had to explain a lot to them." Corbin's group also worked with the natives on a water project that would save carrying water for long distances, would make the water safe to drink, and allow for safer cooking.

In 1993, Corbin spent another two weeks continuing the previous year's work and helping build a medical center. "It took us four hours in a four-wheel drive truck and driving across two rivers to get there, and we would have church at night," he said. During the 1995 trip, Corbin helped obtain Spanish-language Bibles for Hondurans and participated in a project to raise and use tilapia fish to improve the nutrition of the Hondurans.

Another water project in 1997 was particularly successful and satisfying. In telling about the experience, Corbin spoke with moist, reddened eyes. "We were able to put clean water in for thirty-two families. They had been washing their clothes in polluted water," said Corbin. "We just followed the Lord's leading and he took care of things."

Corbin, along with Russ and Patty Boone, traveled to Honduras in 2000 to construct a building with a specially-made kitchen. The kitchen's purpose was to bake special "nutrition bars," which had the appearance of cookies, for the Honduran natives. Their efforts proved to be not only immediately beneficial, but also a sound investment for the natives' future. Today, 22,000 of the nutrition bars are produced every month for the region. The building was expanded, also, to provide a community place to eat and have religious fellowship. Remarkably, much of the financing for the venture came from a source close to Corbin—his deceased father. "I took the Lord's portion of the inheritance to help with the project after he died in 1999," said Corbin.

The missionary work continued through the years, and he watched with glee in 2003 and 2004 when 332 Bibles were acquired for the Lenca Indians of mountainous Honduras, of which thirty-two were of large print for the visually impaired. "We wanted to do something for the people that would last after we were gone," he said. In the last few years, Corbin's main focus has been helping to build an orphanage for the Lenca Indians. Emotionally, Corbin is very close to the project. "It was not too long ago I was like these children, with nothing and no hope. I sincerely hope my tracks on their mountain leaves good memories in these children's minds for many years to come," he said.

Corbin was instrumental in organizing conference in Honduras to teach evangelization skills in the fall of 2007, and a vacation Bible school for the Lenca Indian children is being planned. Looking back at what the wiry built and bearded Corbin would call "God working," he described some of the accomplishments of the missionary work since the early '90s. "We counted 231 people who were saved (made Christian commitments) as a result of being given Bibles. A church we helped start has grown from four people to 145 today." Corbin has seen people fed, children given school clothes, and watched as Hondurans gained new ways of gaining income. Lives thousands of miles from Russell County have improved significantly because of Corbin's noble endeavors. He sees no reason to discontinue the ongoing work.

"God can use the environment you come from to help do His work if we follow His leading," explained Corbin. "He led us to extend His love from the Appalachians to the mountains of Honduras."

For those interested in helping with the work of Doug Corbin,
contact him at: 200 D. Corbin Road, Jamestown, KY 42629.

Trish Ayers

Light from the Darkroom

Even when award-winning photographer Trish Ayers was spending hours creating good work back in the darkroom, she was writing. Not putting words down, on paper, but forming word images, generating a healthy flow of ideas, seeking definitive summations, and finding avenues to express emotional authenticity.

All of these were mental-writing activities, and their products nestled comfortably in her well-developed mind, reminding her of her youthful passion to write. Today, the Berea resident Ayers is so very glad she spent her time in the darkroom so wisely. That's because an injury suffered in 1990, while working on a photography-grant project at Berea College, started Ayers on a unfortunate series of events that eventually forced her departure from a vocation in photography—and very nearly a departure from her life.

"We still, to this day, don't know what really caused it, either a time when a filing cabinet fell towards me and I tried to stop it, or an automobile accident I had about that time," said the Berea resident. "Anyway, one side of my body began to curl up and I developed a constant pain. I couldn't lift things."

Doctors prescribed physical therapy. They told her of good things that would happen if she "trained like she was in the Olympics." Always physically active, including being a runner, she was emboldened until she got no better. "Some of my family members, who hadn't seen me in a while, pinned me down and told me that they could see it wasn't working, that I needed to go back to the doctor and do something different," she said.

Consequently, she was diagnosed with a herniated cervical disk, and in 1991 underwent cervical fusion surgery. Bad luck visited Trish Ayers again when the operation caused damage to the right laryngeal nerve, and possibly the vegas nerve. Her right vocal fold became paralyzed in the midline position and caused a permanent breathing obstruction.

Trish Ayers

A truly dark time in her life was now unfolding. Soon after the breathing problems were manifested, Ayers encountered the beginnings of a seizure disorder, along with serious allergic reactions to specific foods, spices, and artificial food additives. Her life became a series of regular, life threatening events with the always present fear of an inopportune seizure or violent response to something she ate or breathed. By then, in 1992, a formerly happy wife, proud mother of two young daughters with a charmed, and growing, photography career going full bore, was ambushed. Her life would detour to a drastically different, and terribly rocky path.

In an effort to make the bad not as bad, doctors performed a "permanent tracheotomy" on Ayers in January of 1993. A trach tube was placed through a hole in the front part of her neck. But, sadly, her days in the darkroom were over. Her system no longer could handle the chemical fumes, and so the darkroom equipment was unceremoniously sold or given away. In metaphorical terms, though, she would remain in a dark room for many years after.

"I was in depression and didn't often leave the house. There were some people who thought I had died because they didn't see me around anywhere," Ayers remembered. Close by was her breathing equipment, which held the key to continuing to eke out some semblance of living, at least, physically.

Nagged by a sense of guilt and bouts of despair, Ayers reached a crossroads moment of decision. "I was sitting there in my chair, thinking about what would happen to me if I decided not to use my equipment for support," she said. "I knew that it would only take about five minutes for me to die."

But Trish Ayers thought hard about how making that choice would affect those who loved her. "I decided that I wasn't going to bring that kind of guilt down on them," she said. Buoyed also by thinking of her childhood love for writing and her contemplative years in the photography darkroom, she started journaling her thoughts everyday, with an emphasis on her life positives and future dreams. In taking that step, something good happened. The effect was dramatic, both for her and family. "It led to a sort of emotional and spiritual healing and regenerated our family's will for her to get back into society," said Shan Ayers, her husband.

Though limited somewhat by energy level, chances that seizures would happen, and food and smoke reactions, she began to step outside her imposed isolation booth. She prayed for support in her writing. It came in the form of a local Berea writing group, and the experience moved her forward from merely doing solitary journaling to acquiring a passionate and responsive audience ready to give positive feedback.

"With the group's love and acceptance, I started writing essays and poetry," she said. "It was wonderful, and I began to write all the time." Writing plays, part of Shan's role as associate professor in theatre and general studies at Berea College, became a part of Trish's repertoire, too. The couple soon wrote a play together, one later performed on stage. It was called "Circle of Voices," a dramatization of seven Native-American stories. Trish's confidence soared. Afterward, chided good-naturedly by Shan to "write your own play," Trish wrote furiously. The writing group not only supported her work as a playwright, they coveted her advice and encouragement in the uncharted area. She, likewise, became a supporter and mentor to them, a partnership that is still thriving today. Accordingly, several in the group have since had plays published.

After Trish and Shan's literary effort with "Circle of Voices," she began working earnestly on a play about breast cancer, a disease of which her family members were well acquainted. In it, she emphasized the difficulty of those acting as breast cancer care-givers. "LUMPS" was the ninety-two-page result, and it was presented in Lexington for an artist suffering with breast cancer, along with performances at Western Illinois University, Seattle, and Baltimore. Her poetry can be seen in the book collection, *Poetry Women Speak,* and a short story contribution in *The Rocking Chair Reader Family Gatherings.* Continuing her recent successes, she worked for a while with an off-Broadway producer on a possible adaptation of another play she has written. Her story, "Gregory and the Dreamslayer," has been used by counselors to build hope and confidence in young clients. She has received numerous writing awards, and seems poised to gain even more.

Trish Ayers knows that the physical challenges she continues to face won't allow anything she tackles to be easy. But the tough times didn't stop her before, and one might expect it won't in the future. Very truly, she's still holding onto her writing, that light she found shining, years ago, back in the darkroom.

Other Literary Works of Trish Ayers:

The poem, "Dear Girl," part of production, *Mountain Women Rising*; poem also included in *GirlChild Press Anthology,* "Just Like a Girl: A Minfesta!"

The poems, "The Cradle" and "Appalachian Invasion" part of *The New Mummers Writer's Exchange.*

Two plays, *Judging Quilts* and *Granny's Bidding*, selected to be part of the 2007 Quilt Extravaganza Ten Minute Play Festival; *Judging Quilts* placed third in the 2007 Appalachian Writers Josefina Niggli Playwriting Contest.

Poem, "First Day" was published in *Appalachian Women's Journal.*

Pamela Lynch, R.N.

Blanketing the World with Prayer

Led by a petite, energetic woman known as "Pam," an Episcopalian congregation in the suburbs of Louisville is providing encouragement to many downhearted people—all over the world.

The church building, itself, sits peacefully in the midst of a woodland that looks like a well-foliaged island dropped curiously into a sea of stately, suburban homes with beautifully manicured lawns. To get to the church, one must navigate a long and winding paved road, approximately a mile long. That should get you to the parking lot where you'll note a contemporary structure with lots of glass and several older, more traditional buildings nearby.

But Anchorage's Church of the Epiphany is more than a building, of course. It provides the setting for a whole host of caring individuals, mostly ladies and mostly middle-aged, to do the noble work of seeking to ease the suffering of others. Their work is a "healing blanket" ministry, one that has literally touched thousands of lives in the U.S. and internationally. It was started, and is led by, a passionate and resourceful parish nurse at Epiphany—some might call a parish nurse extraordinaire—by the name of Pamela Lynch.

Since Lynch championed the ministry in 2003, over 7000 blankets, along with informative and attractive prayer booklets called "You are Covered with Prayer" have been sent to the sick, the grieving or simply those in need of prayer. Each blanket is "one yard-squared, two-sided with an iron on appliqué of our logo with a simple prayer," Lynch said.

The blankets are special, customized to the needs and preferences of each recipient, and the ministry group members both enter into a discussion, as well as pray, for the person who will receive it.

Unconditional love is the theme. "The intention behind the blankets is that you be healed in mind, body, or spirit. It may apply for someone experiencing grief, loss, divorce, illness, or loneliness. We'll send it wherever it is needed. We don't turn anybody away, and we don't ask for any money," Lynch said.

Lynch started her position as the parish nurse for Epiphany Church in

Pamela Lynch, R.N.

2001. She has seen her position evolve from a twenty-hour work week to forty or more. The congregation counts forty-nine percent of its members over sixty years old, creating an important need to provide services for the sizeable senior population there. She closely follows about eighty to one hundred persons. Included in Lynch's responsibilities are making home visits, advocating for medical patients, finding affordable medicines, establishing a "caring network" within the life of the church, and, of course, overseeing the healing blanket ministry. It consumes plenty of time and energy. "Ministry is not a forty-hour week. My job is to be a counselor, minister, nurse, social worker, and a case manager," said Lynch, who worked as a nurse in hospitals around the Louisville area before coming to Epiphany.

Angie White, who works with the healing-blanket ministry in the church, praised Lynch's service. "Pam practices what she preaches, and she preaches with prayer," White said.

Like Christ's metaphor of faith like a mustard seed, a seemingly small gesture five years ago got the ball rolling on the blanket ministry. The group originated after someone forwarded an email to Lynch. The message told of a church in San Antonio, Texas that made blankets to give away to those who suffered, "with the premise behind it being prayer," Lynch said. At the time, former Epiphany pastor, Father Bill Griner, was suffering from esophageal cancer. Taking the Texas church idea, Lynch initiated a new version of the project and Griner became the first blanket recipient. It was accepted with warm gratitude.

"Father Griner was very appreciative, and as he began to recover, he helped publicize our efforts," explained Lynch. E-mails and phone calls, requesting the "prayed over" blankets, began to pour into the church. A group of eager church members, nearly all women and eventually totaling about 100 strong, met on Thursdays and Saturdays one time per month. Some participants were skilled seamstresses, some were not. The time together became a kind of worship service. Besides bonding with each other by talking and sharing a meal, they spent time talking lovingly of the persons who needed support. They sewed blankets. They prayed that their gesture would bring the warmth of love and the knowledge to the recipients that "you are not alone."

Today, the work is going strong and spreading, according to Lynch. "There now are about 100 churches in the Louisville area who have a similar ministry," she said. "We also know of healing-blanket ministries in Australia, Germany, France and Canada who started doing it because of this church."

Lynch is hopeful for the future. "The healing-blankets ministry has been a 'whole community' blessing," she said. "You'll find both 'liberal' and 'conservative' churches doing it. It crosses all boundaries. It has been like sewing seeds that will someday grow into trees."

A part of Pam Lynch's passion for serving hurt people is because *she* has suffered. She has a healthy, well-adjusted teenage daughter, but she also lost a set of twins to a miscarriage years ago. Besides her work at church, which, she said, "has outgrown me," Lynch works hard to model a spirit of giving with her husband, a youth minister in another Louisville church, and her daughter. "We raise our daughter to give to other people," Lynch said. "Sometimes, we go on vacations together and I just turn my cell phone off in order to concentrate on family time."

It seems there's only so much Pam Lynch to go around. Now, if only there were more servants like her.

Sue Sword

Raising Money and Hope in Appalachia

Sue Sword grew up in Melvin, Kentucky, just outside the mining town of Wheelwright in eastern Kentucky. Friends remember her spunk and caring nature when they watched her as a seventh-grader driving a car while delivering groceries to locals. Born in 1944, she was the oldest of six kids, and people said her family was poor. "We were just a typical eastern Kentucky family," she said. "Everyone else was poor, too. My parents were frugal people, though, and all of us kids went on to college and became successful at what we do."

Truly, no one in her family has excelled any more than Sue. Quietly and with little fanfare, she has used her prolific fund-raising skills and her passion for her native land to attract hundreds of millions worth of cash or in-kind donations through the Christian Appalachian Project organization. Funds have more than tripled since she became CAP's vice-president of development in 1998. In her job, Sword presides over the sending of twenty-four million pieces of mail each year. It's a huge challenge, but it's made a little easier when she sees people's eyes brighten—both those of the care recipients and the benefactors who see their money being used wisely.

CAP is a Kentucky-based, inter-denominational Christian organization "committed to serving people in need in Appalachia (parts of thirteen states) by providing physical, spiritual and emotional support through a wide variety of programs and services." It was founded by Father Ralph Beiting in 1964 and has grown to be the fifteenth largest social services charity in the nation. CAP administers seventy different programs and has about 230 paid em- ployees. Even more impressive, the organization is built on a large number of both long and short-term volunteers dedicated to improving others' living conditions, many of whom live in eastern Kentucky.

Sword gained valuable training in the seeking and handling of great sums of money for the public good before she was hired by CAP in 1998. She worked for former Kentucky governors John Y. Brown and Brereton Jones in economic

Sue Sword

development programs. She directed Jones's international trade department in the 1990s and dealt with the complexities of the North American Trade Agreement (NAFTA). "I enjoyed the work and they were nice men to work for. My father had been involved in politics long ago in the area of mining regulations," she said.

It was pretty heady stuff for a humble mountain girl, especially since economics was not her area of college study. She started out in education, graduating from Morehead State, and taught in Floyd County, Frankfort and Fayette County. Later, she involved herself in the state's career ladder teaching program, and even worked in real estate for a while. She found her true niche at CAP, however.

It's easy to observe her affection for what she does in CAP, even with the hard work, traveling and long hours the job demands. "When I see people noticing their donated money being used well, to help others, and I hear all the 'little stories' of changed lives, that's what makes it worthwhile," she said.

Many would feel refreshed to hear of an honest, authentic voice— one willing to admit mistakes—coming from a charity organization, especially one dealing with such enormous amounts of money and a high profile to keep. Sword believes in total honesty. In her 2005 book Sword authored for CAP, called *And the Rains Came*, she remarked that the organization did not do an optimal job in regard to a 2004 flooding situation in eastern Kentucky and southwest West Virginia. "We know, in the final analysis," she said, "(we) could have been far more responsive and efficient, and that far fewer people would have suffered if we had been better prepared…Our goal is to be ready for the next one because it will surely come. We can't stop floods, but we can be more prepared." Sword makes it plain that the givers' wishes are honored. "We make sure we use the money for what they designate it, plus we never make their names available to other organizations unless they give permission to do it," she said. And, she makes sure donators receives direct notes of appreciation. "We do them daily," she said.

Sword is proud that CAP creates a culture of compassion and values its employees, too. "If one of our employees wants to go to college and can't afford it, we help them," she said. "We care for them." Sword personally has encouraged a number of CAP's employees to aspire for promotions within the ranks. She thinks it is important that employees are invited to attend, and lead, daily devotions that start each day. "We put no pressure on anyone to attend, but a whole lot of them do. This is a Christian organization," she said.

Johnny Thompson, who works closely with Sword at CAP, said she "has a golden heart and strong desire to help people. Her interest has been to do things on a larger scale (to help more people). Growing up like she did, she has seen, for example, what flooding does to lives. She goes outside Appalachia and makes presentations to others about what CAP does." Further, Thompson explained that Sword's effectiveness has a lot to do with her systematic approach to fund-raising. "She studies the industry and has a hunger for information about it. Legislative-wise, she says well-informed and knows people she can talk to about it. "In working with her, we have had a lot of fun and laughs, but she can be very tough, too," Thompson added. "She sometimes can challenge people about doing things right. She is respected by us and others in the industry."

Sherry Buresh, another colleague, also praised Sword. "Sue is a 'walking idea machine,'" she said, "and she gets excited about *your* ideas, too. She has always been there for everyone at CAP."

Sword recognizes that, as her age and priorities change, she will someday see a need to discontinue her work with CAP, but is not sure when it will be. "After all, I didn't plan on being here this long, and my family will always come first. I want to see that all my children and grand-children are happy and secure."

To be sure, Sue Sword has already demonstrated that she has been a Godsend to thousands of other people, and their offspring, too— throughout Appalachia.

"Sue Sword is extraordinary," Buresh said.

Pat Smith

'Building' Dreams for Others

There were more than a hundred central Kentuckians gathered. It was on South Carolina Street, in Gulfport, Mississippi, on Thanksgiving in 2006. The task, besides enjoying a bountiful feast and celebrating the human spirit of compassion, was to build thirteen houses, or maybe more accurately, to lift a bit of new life out of the desolation of Hurricane Katrina.

Some who came were the old regulars who faithfully immersed themselves in Habitat for Humanity projects locally, nationally, even internationally. Dedicated, they continued their good work. There were many who were there for the first time. It was important, each of them thought, to be there—at that place, at that time. They came because they knew Pat Smith, and they wanted to honor him by helping complete the last project he had championed, one that he was en route to oversee on August 27, 2006, when he boarded the fateful Comair Flight 5191 from Lexington's Bluegrass Airport. The fifty-eight-year-old Smith was one of fourty-nine people that day who died in a fiery crash moments after takeoff—considered one of Kentucky's all-time worst human catastrophes.

Pat Smith loved his community. He was, son Brian said, a true "soccer dad" who followed his son throughout his playing days around Lexington, and he served in leadership roles in Christ the King Church and the schools his children, Jennifer and Brian attended. Jennifer talked of the close relationship she had with her father.

159

"We were running partners, three times a week, and did races together," Jennifer recalled about their close relationship. "He always wanted to talk while we were running, but I couldn't walk and talk at the same time. It used to drive him crazy."

But even with the close family ties and his network of friends around central Kentucky, Pat Smith's community was bigger than most people's—much bigger. His community stretched from central Kentucky to America's Deep South and to Mexico, onward to West and South Africa, to

Pat Smith

Northern Ireland and India and Sri Lanka. Smith, sponsored by the worldwide Habitat organization, built "simple, affordable houses," thousands of them, but more importantly, he helped build, and he helped get the best out other individuals' lives.

"There's no way I would have done some of the things I've done without Pat's influence," said Jean Smith, his wife of thirty-seven years. "Like going to places like Ghana on our fiftieth birthday, which was a place with no running water, and helping build mud-brick houses." She told the Lexington-Herald that "Our family's life with Pat was an adventure. He encouraged all of us to stretch what we thought we were capable of and use our God-given talents to be all that we could be." Jean, a normally quiet, more reserved person than Pat, found herself able to speak before groups about her passion for Ghana—a product of Pat Smith's influence, as he often stood next to her. Their marriage exemplified the "team" approach.

Louis Rives, a business partner, lifelong close friend, and one of the few people Pat Smith couldn't seem to cajole into traveling to a distant land to build houses while braving the natural elements, said that even when they were on business trips together, he would often be on the phone, "coordinating some big Habitat projects. He was a compassionate, caring kind of guy who was a practical joker, and he was able to get people to join him on these projects."

Dennis Pike was another close friend of Pat Smith. He participated frequently with Smith on Habitat "builds," most notably international projects in India and Sri Lanka, where the 2004 tsunami catastrophe occurred. Smith led eighty people from Kentucky as they built twenty-six houses in Muzhukkuthurai and other fishing villages in southern India. In a tribute written by Pike in a Habitat newsletter, he called Smith "an ordinary man who did extraordinary things," and he meant it not as a trite platitude. The two climbed Mt. Kilanmajaro in Africa, went on safaris and took adventurous hikes in other places. Smith ran the Chicago Marathon and ran the local Bluegrass 10,000 many times with his daughter Jennifer. Pike marveled as he saw Smith spend three months in India. He noted that Smith made at least fifteen trips to Ghana, and under his guidance built fifty-six houses, a church and a three-room school, as well as a library. After the library was built, Pike remarked that that wasn't enough for his friend. "Pat looked at the completed library and said it needed books, so he arranged to have 3,000 sent from the International Book Project in Lexington," Pike said. When the books arrived in Ghana, the shipment hit a troublesome snag before reaching it's assigned destination. Again, Smith's passion for others and his desire to finish what he started drove him to remedy the situation. He and Pike made a special visit to a commerce official in Ghana to make sure they were delivered to the library. "We drove three hours on a terrible road to get there. Our roads in this country are nothing like theirs." Pike said.

Pike laughed about something Smith often said. "When he would say, 'I've got an idea...' I always wondered what would come next. I knew it was something big."

Lexington Habitat for Humanity executive director Grant Eaton Phelps emphasized the vision of Pat Smith. "Pat's vision was an 'implementable' vision," said Phelps. "He not only came up with the idea, he had the ability to make it work and could share the idea with others.

He was a positive, servant leader who was a humble guy and had tremendous energy." Phelps, who thinks about Smith "every time a plane flies overhead," said that if Smith could come back and talk to each person he knew, he would tell them "to keep building houses, keep up the work."

Smith was held in high esteem even on the international level. He was named Habitat's Volunteer of the Year in 2004. Not surprisingly, Smith donated the money to a fund to send Lexington Habitat staff members on international assignments. Dennis Pike mentioned that Habitat's international board of directors respected him and listened carefully to Smith's recommendations. "They took in consideration the insights he had gained, even if they disagreed on some things," Pike said.

The memory and inspiration of Smith's work will now, in addition, act as an financial investment for building houses. As his daughter, Jennifer, remarked, "Everything was an adventure with Dad." Volunteers in the future will find even more support to follow in Smith's adventurous endeavors of compassion. The Pat Smith Habitat for Humanity Endowment Fund was recently created for that purpose. The fund's goal is to raise a million dollars which will be used to build Habitat houses in Lexington and internationally, with an emphasis in Ghana, plus support habitat's disaster relief projects.

Pat Smith's legacy will live on in the people he touched. The Thanksgiving gathering at Gulfport will always be remembered as special and emotional. "But it was emotional in a good way," said Louis Rives, who attended. People giving, people remembering, people looking to the future with hope and modeled by a life well lived by Pat Smith. As Brian Smith told a reporter at *USA Today,* "At first I thought it was tying up the last chapter of his life, but it's not the last chapter… it's a chapter. It's just a matter of continuing his work."

Afterword

Long before the road trips, the taping and transcribing of interviews for the writing of *Kentucky Heroes* wound down, I figured that exhaustion and a deep longing to finish the project awaited me. It didn't happen that way.

The rides were refreshingly scenic; the interviews were mentally invigorating; the writes—and untold numbers of re-writes—were challenging, but gratifying. I sensed a developing closeness to my family of heroes, enough that my daily time with them will be missed. But, I will be in touch with them frequently, in remembrance and spirit, as I now venture out and share their stories all around Kentucky.

This brings me to the next point...

I will gather more stories of Kentucky heroes for another book similar to this one, and I hope you might be willing to help. After perusing this book, you probably have a good idea of the types of inspirational people I'm seeking. You may contact me via e-mail at steve.flairty@gmail.com. I will read all suggestions and, at least, consider them for inclusion. Thank you in advance for your efforts. You could well be the catalyst that motivates others to higher levels of living.

— Steve Flairty